CAR PAINTING

MATTHEW JONES
AND IAN TAYLOR

THE CROWOOD PRESS

First published in 2015 by
The Crowood Press Ltd
Ramsbury, Marlborough
Wiltshire SN8 2HR

www.crowood.com

British Library Cataloguing-in-Publication Data
A catalogue record for this book is available from the British Library.

ISBN 978 1 84797 947 6

Disclaimer
Safety is of the utmost importance in every aspect of an automotive
workshop. The practical procedures and the tools and equipment
used in automotive workshops are potentially dangerous. Tools should
used in strict accordance with the manufacturer's recommended
procedures and current health and safety regulations. The author
and publisher cannot accept responsibility for any accident or injury
caused by following the advice given in this book.

DEDICATION

I made a bet. I lost. Grace Melville, I cordially dedicate
this book to you (but also to my father and George).

For my father, Ian Taylor.

Designed and typeset by Guy Croton Publishing Services,
Tonbridge, Kent
Printed and bound in Malaysia by Times Offset (M) Sdn Bhd

CONTENTS

PREFACE

Today, automotive painters are in very fortunate position. The products available to them have never been better, both in terms of the final finish and in terms of the preparation process. Every stage is catered for, and every problem will have a solution. This means that keen amateurs that want to try and do the job themselves will have the best possible chance of refinishing their vehicle to a professional standard than ever before.

However, using the products correctly and making a workspace suitable for the job require a lot of preparation and knowledge. This book will tell you what products you need, how to use them, where to use them and what to do when you encounter any problems. It covers the entire process – from discovering the best ways to remove old paint, to panel preparation and on to the spraying process, as well teaching you the ways to ensure your finished vehicle looks better for longer.

It will also tell you how to protect yourself from the process. Painting a vehicle will require you to deal with several extremely toxic chemicals. You will need to learn how to protect yourself from them, the appropriate safety gear to use and a rough guide to current legislation.

Undertaking this job will also involve some local research. You will need to discover how much of the toxic, flammable materials required to undertake the job are allowed to be stored on your premises, how they are stored, what ventilation is required, how you need to dispose of any toxic waste and if you are even allowed to do the job in the place you plan to do it. Your local authority will be able to tell you everything you need to know, but you must make sure you are on the right side of the law before you start work.

Once you have done your research, you can begin repainting your car so it looks like new again.

CHAPTER ONE

ALL ABOUT PAINT

This chapter answers the following questions:

- What paint do I have on my car (water-based, polyurethane, enamel, cellulose or two-pack)?
- What products can I apply to my vehicle (without causing a damaging chemical reaction)?
- How do I select the right colour (implications of a full colour change, colours that hide the most sins, colours that are difficult to maintain)?
- How do I match paint (how to match colours, difficult colours to match, find out what your car's original colour was)?
- How does it all work (paint chemistry basics)?
- Paint and the law – what do I need to know (EU legislation regarding volatile organic compounds or VOCs)?
- Are there any health and safety implications (handling paint, skincare, ventilation)?

Use a white cloth and lacquer thinners to wipe an inconspicuous are of your car's paint to see what kind of paint you have.

Before you can begin to apply paint to your car, you need to start by discovering the chemistry behind the process. This should help inform your spraying technique. It is also essential to know what kind of paint you have on the vehicle as it is this that will determine the extent to which you strip your car. Then there's the law – painting throws up problems that must be addressed and researched before you begin.

FIND OUT WHAT PAINT IS ON YOUR CAR

Knowing what sort of paint your car is finished in will inform how you use this book. Discovering its type is a pretty straightforward process, but it must be done before you begin any work or buy any paint or tools. All you need is a white cloth, some lacquer thinners, 800-grit (or finer) sandpaper and a clean, inconspicuous area of painted bodywork, like the inside of a boot lid. Now dab your cloth with the thinners and rub.

- If colour comes off immediately or the paint begins to wrinkle, you have enamel paint.
- If colour only comes off after a lot of rubbing, you have lacquer paint.
- If nothing comes off, you have urethane paint.
- To see if the finish includes a clear coat, lightly sand a different area. If the dust is white, you have clear coat; if it is the same colour as the car, you do not.

While there is a chance that your car might already have been repainted at some point in its life, it is also worth getting some historical perspective on the sort of finishes that were popular throughout history:

1940s: enamel and lacquer-based paint (quick to apply, requires little finishing after application).

1950s: nitrocellulose paint/lacquer (requires several coats, then a clear coat on top; fast drying, easily correctible and gives a deep, glossy finish).

1960s: urethane and polyurethane paint (quick to dry and apply, durable and easy to correct).

WHAT DOES THAT MEAN?

It's a matter of compatibility. Assuming the surfaces are prepared properly and you spray in the correct conditions (more on that later), you can lay enamel over lacquer. However, if you apply lacquer onto enamel, the surface will almost always wrinkle and get damaged.

The problems are a matter of chemistry – the solvent base for lacquer is far too strong for the softer materials in enamel paint. But compatibility issues do not end there. Paint systems are much like car systems. In the same way that you cannot bolt a Mercedes' cylinder head onto a BMW engine block, there is a good chance you cannot use a BASF thinner with, say, a U-Pol paint; even more so considering increasing health and safety regulations imposed on paint manufacturers. Developers might even change application hardware, like spray guns, and the method of application to meet the required standards, which is an increasing imposition as legislation tightens in Europe.

There is a mass of information about automotive paint and its chemical composition, and you may wish to read more about it, but this book focuses on learning how to apply the paint itself, so the following information is a very brief, very basic guide.

Automotive paint is made up of three basic ingredients:

• Pigments (colour)
• Binders (adherents)
• Solvents (thinners)

It works like this: pigments and binders are solid substances, and solvents allow them to be turned into a liquid and sprayed onto your car. Lacquer paints have lacquer thinners, while enamels and urethanes have reducers; but all of them evaporate, leaving the layer of solid colour on your car.

VOLATILE ORGANIC COMPOUNDS (VOCS)

But along with overspray, it is the solvent evaporation component of the chemical process that causes the most environmental problems and health risks. In 2001, European legislators stepped in to ensure that any paint products that produced significant emissions of 'volatile organic compounds' were regulated. VOCs are defined as any organic compound with an initial boiling point less than, or equal to, 250°C (480°F) measured at a standard pressure of 101.3kPa.

In plain English, a VOC in the world of car painting is a solvent or paint particle that mixes with nitrous oxides and produces ozone. When paint particles or solvents rise into the atmosphere (caused by overspray, which is paint sprayed that does not adhere to the car, and evaporation, respectively), they contribute to air pollution. The European Parliament has stipulated that the VOC content of certain paints and solvents should be 'reduced as much as is technically and economically feasible taking into account climatic conditions'.

Limiting VOC emissions has been the impetus for lots of technical innovation in paint and paint booth-related products. To meet the requirements, paint shops have fitted down-draft ventilation and special air-filtration systems to stop VOCs escaping. Also, a special high-volume low-pressure (HVLP) painting system has been developed that produces 64ft³ per minute of air warmed to 32°C (90°F) at 5lb/in². It means less paint bounces off the car and into the atmosphere, and offers the advantage that you will need to use fewer materials in the process. An HVLP gun can transfer up to 80 per cent from the gun to the bodywork, while a traditional system transfers around 40 per cent, which is barely more than an aerosol can.

Paint itself has also been developed to fall in line with the restrictions, the most notable product being waterborne finishes. As the name suggests, this uses water to suspend the paint pigments and deliver them to the surface to be covered, not solvents. Nearly all waterborne paints use a basecoat colour covered by a clear coat and once it dries, the chemical process is effectively finished. But with traditional finishes, the

This colour chart illustrates the various hues available.

solvent gases continue to work through the surface for up to six months – known as the 'flash time' – which can cause problems if the surface is blocked by anything like detailing and polishing waxes.

It sounds like an excellent solution – and in terms of environmental impact it is a vast improvement – but it is not without fault. Despite reduced VOC levels, waterborne paint has plenty of lethal chemicals in it, so you need a respirator on at all times. It is also slow to dry, expensive and requires special materials for you to apply it (there will be more on this later).

Luckily, most major paint manufacturers sell a low-VOC, solvent-based coating that meets all the legal requirements. Also, you can buy chemical additives for some solvent-based paints that alter it so that it complies with VOC content.

If you are determined to create a finish as original as possible, you will be pleased to learn that the European Parliament has also allowed member states to grant individual licences for limited sales of products that do not meet the VOC criteria. It stipulates that it must be 'for the purposes of restoration and maintenance of buildings and vintage vehicles designated by competent authorities as being of particular historical and cultural value'. That generally means the materials will be expensive, but useable for the DIY enthusiast and useful if you want to complete a faithful restoration.

COLOUR SELECTION

The fastest way to get a steer on your car's colour is to consult the Vehicle Identification Number (VIN) plate, which is a small tag located on your car. Its location varies from car to car, so it is best to consult a car club or enthusiast to advise you. Deciphering this, and discovering which section of the VIN code relates to paint code, depends on the manufacturer. In the absence of an expert, copy all the numbers and letters down, then take it to a paint shop to decode.

But be careful – someone may have changed the car's colour during its lifetime. It is also possible that it has been incorrectly tagged at the factory, though unlikely. As a fail-safe, it is a good idea to tell the paint supplier the basic colour of your paintjob – red, blue, green, etc. – and they will be able to tell if you if it matches up to the code before it is mixed in bulk.

Unfortunately, the complications and scope for error do not end there. If you are painting a more modern classic, there may be several formulas that are quoted for any one colour. It is caused by the automated paint process at the factory – at the production line a batch of, say, twenty cars will be painted one colour, then machines will be cleaned and they will spray the next twenty cars in a different colour. Very slight contamination from other colours and cleaning agents can cause variations from the colour as it appears in the tin.

Black is one of the hardest colours to paint perfectly as it reflects everything.

This is not much of an issue if you plan to fully repaint your car, but if you are attempting a localized repair, it is important that it is matched as closely as possible. Sometimes the car's position on the line – and subsequent variation in paint colour – is listed in the paint code in up to ten different variations; other times it is not at all. If not, find the prime colour and check at a paint shop to see if they have colour chips that show the variations, then match up accordingly.

If you have single-stage or two-stage paint, you also have the option of using a spectrometer – it is the size of a shoebox and has a port on one end that shines a light on the surface, takes a very sophisticated reading of each wavelength of light reflected off the object and works out what colour it is. It is an expensive piece of kit, it requires you to send off a sample section, like a petrol-filler flap, and you will not be able to use it on more complicated finishes like metallics, but it does give a very accurate reading.

CHOOSING A NEW COLOUR

If you are fully repainting your car, you have the option of choosing an entirely new colour. But undertaking a full colour change will greatly increase your workload – more of the car will have to be taken apart, such as the engine if the bay is finished in body colour, as

well as the whole interior if there are any un-trimmed sections. Also, in the world of classic cars, values are profoundly affected by originality, and any deviation from it may have implications for your vehicle, regardless of the colour's desirability. If you do change it over, you will also need to inform (in UK) the Driver and Vehicle Licensing Agency (DVLA). Also remember that some insurers may refuse you cover, and it may invalidate any policy you already have in place on your car or increase the annual premium. Speak to your policy provider beforehand to check.

Then there is the matter of difficulty: it is more difficult to achieve a flawless finish with certain flat colours. Black, for example, reflects everything, highlighting the most minor imperfections in the sheet metal. This is especially challenging if you need to make repairs to the panel; even more so if welding is involved, because every slight ripple – however small – will be painfully obvious.

Bolder finishes like metallics are also troublesome for the novice. While their manufacture has improved exponentially since their inception in the sixties, you have to ensure even application.

Pearl additives are also challenging for beginners. They give a flat colour an additional tint so, when viewed from different angles, the colour changes slightly. TVR famously painted the Sagaris with multi-

Avoid metallic if it is your first time painting.

Because they tend to reflect less than most, colours such as silver and beige are ideal for the first-timer.

stage flip pearl. The effect is created using oxide pigments to milaceous iron oxide (mica) or aluminium. These tiny specs can be painted on one side and left clear on the other. As well as the similar problem of even application, it is difficult to achieve an identical tint across the car, and it will be hard to fade in and repair afterwards.

If this is the first time you've painted a car, you're opting for a full colour-change and you want the finish to look as good as it possibly can, the colours that hide the most sins tend to reflect the least, but they don't tend to be very popular. These are:

- Grey
- Beige
- Silver
- Gold.

CHAPTER TWO

GETTING STARTED

This chapter answers the following questions:

- What kit do I need to paint my own car (all the materials, equipment and supporting products required for the job, beginning to end)?
- How do I build a spray booth (all the requirements for building somewhere suitable for paint finishing)?
- Do I need to repaint my whole car (localized paint work vs. full car)?
- Do I need to plan the job (how to write and order a comprehensive job sheet, and stick to it)?

There are literally thousands of different options of materials and products to choose from. Make sure you make the right decision for your workspace. And prepare to be surprised — even a humble garage can be transformed into a paint booth.

GETTING STARTED

As with any specialist job, even understanding the impenetrable language of the tools required is a bit of a challenge, and if you get the wrong kit it will seriously impede your progress, or the quality of the finished product. They can also be fiendishly expensive, and if you are only planning to paint one or two cars, it might be a more economically viable option to rent some of the larger equipment. However, some supporting products like the paint gun itself are worth splashing out on — even in the same product

line, there are very slight variations that mean you have to 'learn' individual products' idiosyncrasies. We will talk in more detail about guns in later chapters, but first you have to prepare your work space.

HOW TO TURN YOUR WORKSPACE INTO A PAINT BOOTH

Regardless of where you live or what resources fall to hand, you can paint your car yourself. But to make the best of the job there are a few rules of engagement.

First – space. You do not need much, but you do need some. Make sure you can manoeuvre your vehicle so there is at least three metres of room around every panel at all times: you will need to keep your paint gun at between fifteen and twenty centimetres from

Even small spaces can be transformed into a workable paint shop, but there are some minimal requirements.

What you do not remove will have to be carefully stored.

whatever you are painting at all times, and be able to move yourself up and down easily at all times with your elbow bent, so this is a good safe minimum.
Second – surfaces. Dust and dirt particles are the enemy here, so dirt and gravel floors are out. You will also need a flat bench on which to mix your paint, and none of it can intrude on your painting area.
Third – ventilation. As long as you can leave the door through which you have brought your vehicle open, you should be fine.
Finally – power. You are going to need to run a fresh-air respirator compressor, air compressor, a large fan and lots of lights, so you must have good access to a mains plug.

If your place fits the bill, you can now start work on making it into a paint booth. Here is what you need to do to begin the transformation:

• Deep-clean your workspace. This should not be a quick job – you will inevitably have stored things that have got dusty. Box them away and move them out for a day. Dust everywhere with the door open, sweep the floor, vacuum extensively, then scrub the walls and floor down with soapy water.

• Now you have a clean garage. If you have not managed to bin most of your old belongings, arrange them as efficiently as possible around the walls or, ideally, stow boxes and storage crates in some roof space. If your storage containers contain anything likely to leak, like liquids, make sure that they are wrapped in plastic to ensure nothing drips down.

• Before you roll your vehicle into your workspace, position your equipment as efficiently and logically as possible. So long as your power lines are long enough, you can put some of the bulky items that you will need to get hold of – like compressors – outside; that way you avoid tripping over them and it will liberate more indoor space.

• You can never have too much lighting when you paint a car – you will need to have at least one large, bright light in each corner of your garage, prefer-ably two at each end, two more on each side of the middle of your space and four overhead, spaced evenly across the roof area. It may be more cost-effective to rent a set of telescopic lighting rigs (or, if space is tight, some tasklights) than buy them. Remember that all lights should be fire-proof (paint is extremely flammable).

HEAT LAMPS

The ideal temperature to paint in is between 15 and 20°C (60 and 68°F). If your workspace is much colder, moisture will find its way into the paint. When the paint dries, moisture will remain beneath it, and bubble up causing microblistering. If your workspace is too warm, the paint will not be able to flow properly, as it will dry too quickly, which will give the finish an orange-peel effect.

Where weather conditions vary, you will need to maintain and stabilize the temperature with some form of heating. Avoid propane space heaters as they produce a naked flame and they have a fan component that will blow dust and other contaminants onto your freshly painted panel. If your garage is not centrally heated, use infrared heating lamps, as there is no naked flame. Prices range from around £130 for a small unit to £2,000 for a multi-lamp setup, but they are available to hire.

Heat lamps will help you to moderate the temperature in your workspace.

WHEN IT COMES TIME TO PAINT

- If you have a driveway in front of your garage, make sure it is thoroughly wet before and during the time you are painting – this keeps dust ingress to a minimum.
- If you paint inside, do not wet your floor down, just make sure it is very clean. If you put water in an enclosed area it will add humidity to the air, which could affect the way the paint adheres to your panel.
- Regardless of how neat you are, you will get speckles of paint overspray everywhere. The best and most cost-effective solution is to line your workspace walls with clear plastic sheeting, which you can buy by the roll from DIY shops. Roll an edge of it around some long, thin strips of wood and drill them into the ceiling or beams next to your walls. Drape down the plastic and attach it to the floor with duct tape. You'll need to line the ceiling, too, but make holes for hanging light fixtures and remove any precious shades – they will get covered in paint.
- For the section of sheeting in front of the workspace's entrance, you will need to weigh down the lower edge of your plastic and cut a hole for your ventilation fan. The former stops dust and debris floating in and disrupting your paintwork. Just in case your fan accidentally gets set from suck to blow, tape a lint-free cloth to the blade guard. Once you have set up your sheeting inside, you should not be able to see any daylight between the fan and plastic. If you can, seal it up with duct tape.

RESPIRATION

When you are preparing your car for paint, you will be exposed to several damaging chemicals, and you have to protect yourself from them. You should also make sure that whatever you buy is fit for purpose. Here is a guide to what is on offer. Because of the toxicity of paint and the supporting materials you will use, it is best to opt for products that offer more protection than you think you might need. These products may be more expensive, but think of them as an insurance policy.

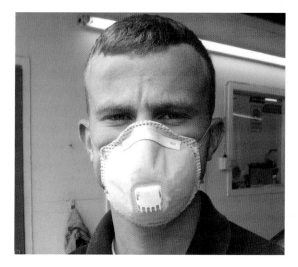

An N95 disposable fibre respirator will not be enough for a full paint job.

N95 RESPIRATOR

This is a disposable type with a fibre cover that goes over your mouth. This, categorically, isn't suitable for painting a car, but it will just about do for sanding work. If you are allergic to latex, make sure it says 'hypoallergenic'.

HALF-FACE RESPIRATOR

Unlike the N95, you can use this for painting, but it does not offer the best protection. It is wider than the N95 and has two filter cartridges to keep air as clean as possible. You will be able to use this for sanding as well as painting, but you will need to use goggles as well.

FULL-FACE RESPIRATOR

As the name suggests, it covers your entire face. And if you value your eyes and lungs as much as you should, it's the one to go for. Remember, the chemicals you'll be working with are pretty aggressive. There are two types: mechanical and electrical. The electrical ones are also known as supplied air respirators, which are best for enclosed environments like yours. They have a separate unit that filters out the nasty stuff. Opt for a battery-powered one – they're cheaper and offer around 20 minutes of filtration between charges. This should be plenty if you paint a car one panel at a time.

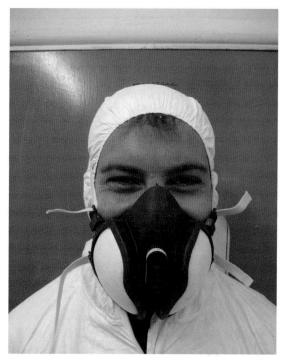

A half-face respirator is the minimum requirement for painting.

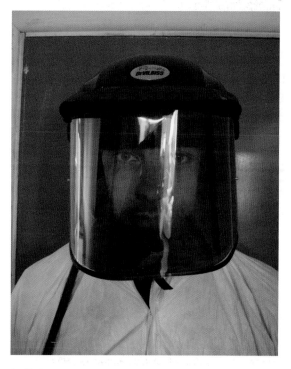

Full-face respirators are the safest option.

When you are buying or renting any sort of protective respiration product, you should make sure that the nose cup seal is air-tight, otherwise you risk inhaling toxic fumes, and the lens may fog up. Make sure you have found out if there are any problems long before you start painting.

GLOVES

It may seem like overkill, but gloves are essential. First, chemicals can get in through your pores, and second, cleaning paint off your hands is a horrible chore, especially if the only products you are using to do so are domestic shower gels and soaps. Latex surgery gloves are best because they are cheap and tight-fitting: they allow a lot more feel than heavy-weight industrial gloves, which is important when performing the delicate task of metering your spray gun. If you use thick, heavy material gloves, you also risk introducing lint motes to your freshly-painted panel. Also, they reduce feel drastically. Just as you would with your mask, make sure you get hypoallergenic gloves if you have an allergy to latex. It is very important that the gloves fit, but not too tightly, because they could split and expose your skin.

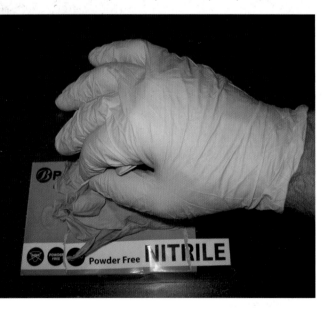

Do not forget to protect your hands with latex gloves.

OVERALLS

As well as gloves, you will need a set of overalls. However, you must not use normal mechanics' heavy-duty cotton products. They will not offer your skin much in the way of protection because they tend to be a loose cut with large gaps around the cuffs and ankles. Because of the material they are made from, loose lint may drift off them and onto your panel, too. This will create vast amounts of unnecessary work for you during the final finishing phase of your paint job, and may mean you have to repaint an entire panel. Two breathable, hooded, disposable coveralls should be enough protection for every vehicle you paint – they will insulate you from toxic spray mist and will not shed any lint. Make sure they have got elasticized cuffs, ankles and hood surrounds. You can get them in various sizes, though it is best to go for a generous fit. However, too loose and you may get airlines tangled or, worse, accidentally rub them on wet paint.

COMPRESSOR

Regardless of how clean your workspace is and how well you have prepared your vehicle, an old compressor that is either too small or full of moisture and oil deposits could ruin your paint finish and spray gun. They can be expensive, though, so renting is a good option unless you want to use air tools regularly. Your compressor should be at least 5bhp, which should enable you to charge it with air and use it without the compressor running constantly – if the compressor is always running it will get hot, which can cause condensation in the air line and mix water into your paint, ruining the finish with fisheyes. It is also worth remembering that some larger compressors may require 220V wiring.

Deciding on the compressor's tank capacity is dependent on your budget, but go for something as big as you can afford. Anything above 100ltr should allow you to paint a car without having to recharge your air supply in the middle of a job.

To work out how powerful your compressor needs to be (which is measured in the cubic feet per meter of air it can move, or cfm), you will need to consult your chosen paint gun's requirements.

CAR PAINTING

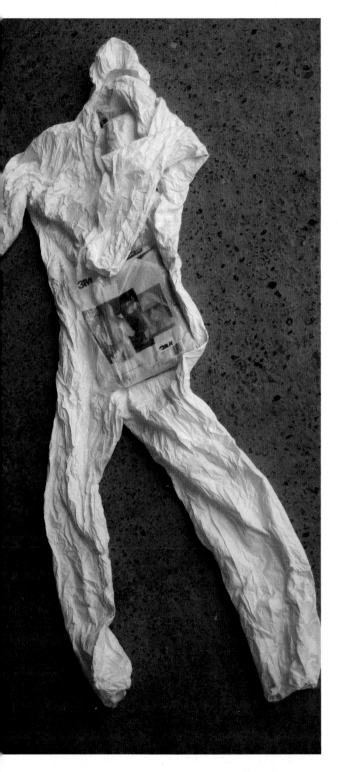

Order the way you put your overalls on to make life easier.

Mechanics' overalls are not up to the job. Use dedicated equipment like this 3M suit.

Suiting-Up

You will need to put on your materials in the following order to ensure the best possible protection:

1 Disposable overalls
2 Gloves
3 Tape the wrists of your overalls up so no excess material drags across your panels – use masking tape
4 The overall hood, making sure your neck and head are fully covered
5 Respirator

Make sure your compressor comes with a dry-air system to stop moisture being introduced to the tank. They include a dryer that cools the air to separate it from any water, and then filters the water from the air. Without it the paint will become contaminated when it lands on the surface. External dry-air systems are also available, and there are several guides that detail different ways to build your own online.

DRY-AIR ADDITIONS

Before even looking at your spray gun, you need to ensure you have an appropriate air supply that is as free of any moisture as it can be, otherwise small droplets will mix with the paint and ruin the finish on your panel. When air gets drawn into the compression circuit, it is squashed to twelve times its normal pressure. Moisture in its vapour state — from the humidity in the air around us — will condense. As the condensed air moves through the system it will slowly cool causing more condensation, adding more and more moisture to the air lines it passes through.

When the time comes to paint your car, rent a compressed air aftercooler, which cools air to approximately 10°C above ambient temperature, causing the water vapour in the compressed air to condense and be collected in a separator, and removing it from your air supply. Used in conjunction with an in-line filter – fitted after the aftercooler in the circuit – your compressed air quality will be extremely high, which gives your paint the best possible finish. As with all your tools and equipment, it is advisable to find the best possible products and materials, and make sure everything is of the highest quality to make sure you have the highest chance of getting the job right first time around.

RENTING A PROFESSIONAL SPRAY BOOTH

If you – or your significant other – would prefer it if you did not convert your garage into an impromptu paint shop, there are alternatives – like renting. Thanks to increasing legislative requirements, like downdraft ventilation, overspray capturing mechanisms and paint disposal management, professional paint booths are an expensive commodity. To offset the costs some bodyshops make theirs available for hire, usually under supervision. There are obvious advantages – lots of room, no tedious legalities to concern yourself with, and the fact that it is a professional spray booth. However, there are drawbacks to consider:

• Factor in the price of disassembly and preparation, or budget for transportation costs. And remember, you cannot tow a stripped, ready-to-paint car out in the open on the road unless the weather is anything other than bone-dry.
• There will not be much leeway in your allotted time slot. Take too long and you will be charged extra or your car may be pushed outside before it is ready. At home you will be more focused, working at a pace you are comfortable with and stand a far greater chance of enjoying yourself.
• The basic rental rate may not include a supervisor, materials or equipment. Make sure all quotes have no hidden extras.
• You will have to adjust your insurance policy if you are transporting the vehicle and leaving it at a business address. This may carry an additional cost. Your policy may also be invalid if you do not inform your provider.

What You Will Need in Brief

• Extraction fan running at least 9,000cfm
• Plastic sheeting
• Fresh-air respirator
• Lint-free cloth
• Two rolls of duct tape
• Some long, thin bits of wood (old lath works well)
• Drill
• Screws
• Additional lighting rigs

A professional spray booth is ideal if you can find a tame paint shop owner, but renting one has its drawbacks.

MATERIALS

Now you have your space arranged, you need to start ordering in some materials. Specialist products for individual jobs will pop up as we go along, but these are the basic components required for a simple paint job.

Also, before we get stuck in, it is important to revisit a point we mentioned in Chapter 1 – paint manufacturers sell systems, not individual products, and everything is designed to be chemically compatible – from degreasers through to the paint itself. Speak to your supplier and they can advise the right tools for the job. Do not be afraid to tell them that you have little or no painting experience because everything from the gun you use to the workspace you plan to undertake the job in can have implications on the best product for you.

With that in mind, here are the bare bones of your shopping list:

• Degreaser
• Tack cloths
• Masking tape
• Masking paper
• Thinner
• Paint strippers
• Primer
• Sealers
• Stripers and strainers
• Body filler
• Production paper
• Wet and dry paper

Now you're ready to strip your car back.

CHAPTER THREE

UNDRESSING YOUR CAR

This chapter answers the following questions:

- How do I know what my car is painted with?
- How do I begin stripping down my car?
- What are the best ways to remove my old paint?
- How much paint should I remove?
- What are the options and how long will it take?

You have your workspace ready and your products on hand – now is the time to get to work on your vehicle. Each car will need to be treated differently with regards to stripping, and the extent to which you remove parts and paint will depend on the type of job you plan to do. However, whatever it is you have planned, the fun really begins now.

GET TO KNOW YOUR CAR AND WHAT PROBLEMS IT HAS

Good paint and bodywork finishes always lie in the preparation. As we have already mentioned, the actual painting component is a tiny percentage of the job, and this should not be underestimated. But before you can begin to prepare your car, you have to diagnose the problems themselves, as well as work out the best course of action based on your findings. Some of the ways you deal with bodywork woes are a matter of personal preference, while others have a definite right/wrong approach. But before you work out what to do, you have to undress your car first.

It is essential to get to know your car's woes so you can work out an accurate timeframe.

The more parts you strip, the better your paint job will be. Simple as that!

REMOVING PARTS

The more parts you remove, the better quality your paint finish will be – it is as simple as that. At the factory, the metal shell will have been painted with no parts on it, and this is what you should try and aim for with your paint job, time and funds permitting. You will also avoid getting any overspray or aggressive chemicals on components or trims that may be costly to replace, or time-consuming to remove paint from. Also, should you reach a point where you wish to sell the car, buyers may also notice things like overspray and concerns may arise over the quality of the finish and what lurks underneath the shiny top coat. This will affect the value greatly.

To avoid any of these problems, you will have to remove all exterior trim as a bare minimum. Get a copy of your car's technical manual, or find a factory repair manual – often available from dealerships if it is a more modern vehicle. While a lot of the manuals supplied with cars only study the basics – especially on more modern models – they may give you useful insights on things like lens and trim removal, as this often falls under the basic servicing and maintenance subjects this literature was designed to guide.

Also, it is advisable to join a model-specific car club and seek advice for removal procedure, even if there are manuals available. Clubs are a mine of information, and if you get stuck you will generally find a group of enthusiastic experts on hand to help. For more unusual vehicles, you may find no such club exists, but you should broaden your search online. You will almost always find a message board or forum website dedicated to your car, which will be populated with like-minded enthusiasts.

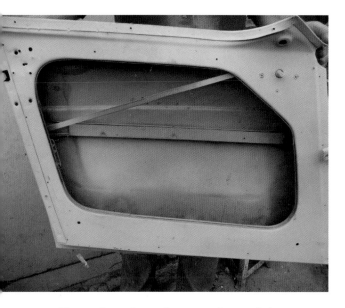

Try and get doors down to a bare minimum too.

Before you take a spanner to your car, make sure you have lots of old, hard-wearing boxes. Use some masking tape and a pen to label them, and everything as it comes off – whether it is driver's side or passenger's side, front or back – and make a note of any specific removal requirements ready for re-fitment. It is also easier to thread small nuts and bolts back onto parts after removal to avoid losing anything and for ease of fitment when the time comes. Take this opportunity to clean up any dirty or rusty threads, and add a small dab of grease to ease the process when you come to reassemble.

You will notice that most exterior parts on older cars are fastened using nuts, bolts or screws – even badges and emblems. Make sure you inspect the back of the panel it is fitted to carefully so you can work out how it is supposed to be removed. On things like door trim, this will require you to strip down the door cards inside for proper access, which are usually held on with plastic clips. They will rarely be visible from the outside, and often require prising off, but make sure you have stripped off any door handles or arm rests beforehand, usually secured with Philips screws accessed from underneath the part. There may be caps to cover them, so use a small flathead screwdriver to gently lever them off.

It can be tempting to over-strip though, especially around doors. Removing handles and trim rarely requires you to remove the entire winder or lock mechanism, for example, so make sure you have carefully checked every access point and angle before you strip anything back.

Grilles are notoriously tricky to remove, and will require careful study. Always look from the inside, and do not remove all the screws and bolts you can see without checking you absolutely need to – often manufacturers build them so they can be taken out as one piece, with various trims, badges and their fixtures remaining in place.

Headlights are generally fastened with screws in the back of their housing – some plastic covers may need to be removed for access depending on the age of your car. Do not unscrew anything with springs beneath them, as they generally are used to adjust the light beam direction. Rear light clusters are almost always removed from inside the boot as a unit, but on some older vehicles you will need to remove the lenses separately before you can access and remove the assembly behind.

Bumpers can be difficult on older cars as nuts and bolts are often left unprotected and exposed to the

Grilles are usually fastened from the back with hidden nuts and bolts.

Avoid unscrewing anything with a spring, as it will probably be an adjuster not a fastener.

Larger bumpers may require you to use a jack or axle stand to avoid dropping them.

elements. To avoid snapping bolts, use penetrating oil liberally, if you can, and leave it to soak in overnight if fastenings are hard to remove. They can be heavy too, especially chrome items, and may require support with a jack or axle stand when you are stripping them so they do not fall on you, and to ensure none of the threads are damaged by removal at strange angles. The best way to remove them is to recruit a friend to remove one side, supporting the weight as they go, while you do the same on the other side. You should be able to slide it off without damaging the part. Chrome parts tend to be costly to replace and repair, so be extremely careful with both removal and storage.

Some bumpers and all panels designed to open and close will have weather protection on them, in the form of a seal or gasket. They are usually rubber and are often held in place with metal or plastic retainers or adhesive. To check how they are fitted, gently prise up the part and look at the back of it, but be careful – some parts may be brittle. You may be able to re-use a lot of these parts, so study their condition carefully. Any rubbers with cracks in should be replaced to stop water ingress, though. If your budget permits, it is worth replacing any older rubbers as a matter of course, as an insurance policy. This will prevent water ingress, which will serve to protect your paint job, and the chrome parts themselves. Bumpers and other trims tend to be very costly to replace or repair.

WHERE TO START

In previous chapters, we told you how to work out what kind of paint you have on your car. But unless you bought the car new or had a close relationship with the person that did, you will not know what is lurking under the top coat. Old cars have a history, that is why we like them so much, but with history comes the odd skeleton in the closet that will not necessarily be obvious until you start peeling away the layers – whether it is a poor professional repaint or localized repair undertaken on a budget, it is important to know what you are working with, as this will affect the quality of your finished product. So, what to do?

PAINT DEPTH GAUGE

Measure the depth of paint with one of these little gizmos to tell how many times – or if at all – your car has been under the gun. The tool measures the distance between the paint's surface and the metal below. Magnetic versions are the cheapest at around £40, though a more reliable ultrasonic model with a digital readout is the most accurate, but will cost around £550. They do only work on steel-bodied cars, and are not always 100 per cent reliable, but they will you give you a good idea.

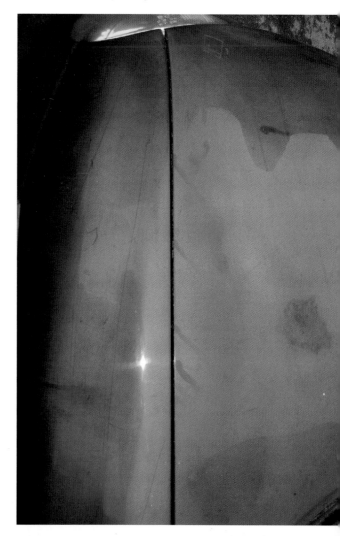

Some paint can be restored with compounds. Original is best.

LEAVE THE ORIGINAL PAINT

If the car has never been repainted, and you are absolutely sure of its provenance, and the surface is not peeling or cracking, painting over the original finish is a far less time-consuming option (that is assuming it cannot be refreshed – turn to Chapter 13 for a guide to paint rejuvenation). Remember that when it was painted originally, it would have been done so in the best possible conditions. On a paint thickness gauge, original finishes measure between 0.003in and 0.005in (0.0762 and 0.127mm) thick. Any more than 0.005in, and there is a good chance your car has been sprayed at some point.

LOCALIZED STRIPPING

If a car has any signs of previous repairs or damage, you should strip those areas back to bare metal. The quality of workmanship and products available have changed dramatically over the last forty years (remember, it was once an acceptable practice to repair entire floors with body filler and newspaper), and knowing what is under paint, however well executed it looks, is essential for a good, long-lasting finish. Cars that have been painted post-factory can measure up to 0.015in (0.381mm) thick with a gauge, and at that thick-

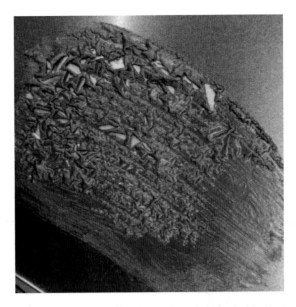

Painting a car does not always mean painting the whole thing.

ness there is a very good chance new paint will crack because the different substrates underneath will expand and contract at different rates.

COMPLETE BARE METAL

Starting with naked steel, and knowing exactly what you are tackling, is by far and away the best baseline to work from – you will not have to

Bare metal is the best starting point for a paint job.

worry about substrate expansion and contraction, or chemical reaction, and you can paint every single area – engine bay, interior exterior – so there is no risk of compromising the uniformity of colour. However, bare metal does require considerably more work. That said, it does not necessarily mean scrubbing off every pigment by hand, and there are several cheap and environmentally responsible modern techniques you can use to remove all the old finishes.

STRIPPING

Getting rid of old paint generally involves one of two methods – mechanical or chemical. The former relies on scraping or blasting off the paint, the latter relies on applying a product that does the hard work for you. Both are suitable for DIY painters, and both have their advantages and pitfalls. For the best possible results, you should familiarize yourself with each method, and use both depending on the job in hand. However, first you have to decide how you will tear the car down.

THE DRY BUILD

Some people will prefer to rehang panels removed for prep before the car is painted (this is known as the dry build), while others chose to do so after the spraying work has been finished. However, while painting each panel when it is removed from the bodywork ensures exceptional material coverage, space constraints may affect your ability to spray your vehicle at the same time in the same place.

This level of stripping is recommended, but will make more work for you.

Sanding is fast, but should by no means be the only method you use to strip paint.

If you are a novice, you should also consider how much you could be risking your paint job during reconstruction. Chances are, you will need to spend a fair amount of time working on the fitment of panels, which may include rubbing two panels together. Obviously, this can also damage fresh paint.

Finally, there is the simple matter of over-complication. If you just plan to respray the outside of your car and you have no alignment issues, this will make a great deal of extra work for you. While you can only achieve the best possible paint finish by stripping your vehicle back to bare metal, it may not always be practical to do so, so long as you limit your expectations along with your workload.

MECHANICAL

First of the mechanical processes is sanding. It is the easiest way to get started, and you can see some real progress quickly. It also means you do not have to disassemble the car to quite the same extent as you would if you stripped a panel chemically or blasted it. However, stripping an entire car by hand with sandpaper will take a tremendous amount of time and energy, even with a power sander.

Power sanders come in two main types: rotary and dual-action (DA). A rotary sander generally has a circular paper disc that is attached to the machine and spins quickly, so it cuts through the paint more quickly. However, you will need to exercise some caution – if you dwell too much on a single area, you may clog the paper, burn the paint as opposed to remove it or even warp the metal underneath by generating too much heat on the surface. DA sander heads move in two different directions, so the cutting process is aggressive, but more controlled. It will take longer to strip the panel, but you stand less chance of warping the panel or scratching the metal beneath too deeply.

The big advantage of sanding is that you can control how aggressive it is, even with a rotary power sander. Sandpaper comes in a variety of coarsenesses or grits – the lower the number, the rougher the paper and the more paint it will cut through. For stripping down to metal, 80 grit is a good starting point. Moving down to 40 will help tougher finishes and as low as 24 for the really recalcitrant stuff. But be careful – low-grit sandpaper can mark or gouge steel, and that will require additional filler work before you

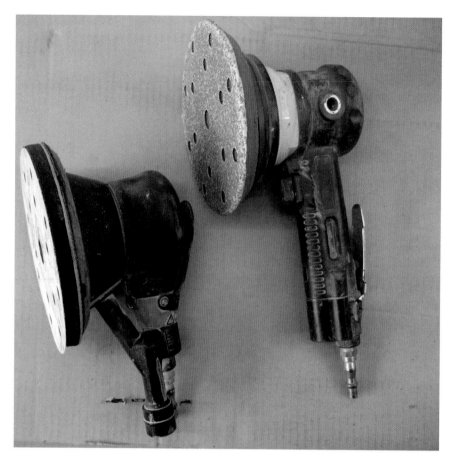

Power sanders will cut through paint quickly but you must exercise caution when you use them.

It might be fiddly, but you can strip some errant paint with a razor blade.

If you want to see quick results, blasting is the way to go.

are ready to lay down your primer coats. Minimize this where you can – clean bare metal that is dent- and scratch-free is the very best starting point for a paint job, and should be what you aim for throughout the stripping process.

If you have a particularly poor paint job on your car, you can try removing it with a razor blade. This technique only applies to cars that have been repainted badly, where the material has not properly stuck to the substrate underneath. Even the worst factory finishes will have adhered to some degree. Remove it as you would a sticker by catching an edge of the bad paint, then encour- aging it off the surface using a combination of gentle pulling and shaving. You will have to use other methods in conjunction with this, but it is a good starting point and will save you a great deal of work as well as minimizing damage to the surface metal underneath.

BLASTING

Blasting falls under the mechanical category, but it is a very different process – it involves sand, or a sand-like media, being blasted onto the paint work with compressed air. Like sanding, there is an element of choice in its aggressiveness, though you will need specialist equipment and a bit of practice to get it right – you can damage the metal underneath if you are too heavy handed or use the wrong media, and there is a fair bit of clean-up to deal with afterwards, so it is not suitable for every work space.

Baking soda is the softest of the blast media and will cut back ordinary paint without too many risks of damaging the metal underneath. It's also good for cars made out of anything softer than steel, like fibre- glass or aluminium. The soda also dries out the metal underneath, so, providing your panel does not come into contact with water or is stored in a particularly moist garage, you can leave it undressed for a few days

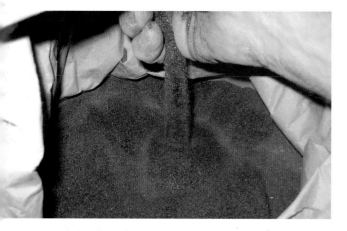

Opt for a gentle blast medium. Soda is very good.

without too much risk of rust setting in in earnest. You will have a fair bit of cleaning up to do afterwards. Removing can also be difficult with soda – because it is gentle, it cannot cut through much old paint, nor can it cope with large amounts of body filler, so if you have a particularly ravaged panel, it is probably better to leave it to a more aggressive medium.

Non-soda media is rated according to its size. The lower the number, the smaller the particle size and the less damage it is likely to inflict on the metal underneath. Stick to 12 (0.004in/0.1016mm) for easy work, moving up to a maximum of 40 (0.0016in/0.0406mm) if you have a lot of corrosion to get through.

Another consideration is blasting pressure. Media is shot at anything between 200 and 400mph (320 and 640km/h), so you need to be sure you prevent unwanted body damage to you and your panel when you undertake the job. It also means there are certain requirements for your air compressor – a chart with detailed information should be available at all shops selling media, but if you need to blast 7ft³ per minute at 80psi and you have a ³/₃₂in nozzle, for example, your compressor needs to be good for between 2 and 3bhp.

It is also worth remembering that there are also some ingredients in certain media that can cause you problems. Silica, for example, will do your lungs no good at all, and you should only ever use it while wearing respiratory equipment. Read more about choosing the right equipment in Chapter 2.

CHEMICAL STRIPPING

Another route to naked metal is using a chemical stripper to remove old paint. There are no risks of pitting and warping the surface underneath, and it removes everything down to the metal (apart from filler). All you do is brush it on the surface – it is best to score the paint first with a sharp knife so the chemicals can find as many ways in to the paint as possible. Wait for it to work – usually around 20 minutes, though products do vary, then scrape off the residue with a sharp-edged tool. It is best to use something made of plastic or nylon to avoid scratching the paint below.

Make sure you use a respirator when using paint strippers as the fumes are highly toxic.

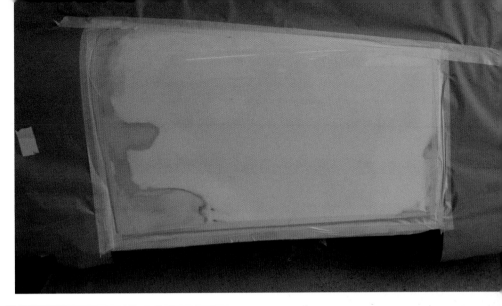

Mask off seams before applying chemical paint stripper so the agent does not get trapped and leak onto your fresh paint.

Using this method, and a product like Nitromors, a full car should take around two days, and around 10ltr of stripper. The chemicals themselves take from ten minutes to a few hours to work, and their effectiveness varies dramatically depending on the age and thickness of the paint, but is generally a lot less labour-intensive than sanding.

However, there are some important considerations to make when using chemicals. All of the stripper will need to be removed before you can prepare the body for paint, and it can easily find its way into your bodywork's seams – the areas of folded metal. After time, any chemicals not removed from there will trickle out onto your new paint. The best way to avoid this is by masking off the seams before brushing on the stripper, then stripping them mechanically with a sander or abrasive wheel.

It has its disadvantages, too. Scraping chemical stripper off a car can cause some gouges to the metal underneath, and most strippers will require neutralization or rinsing afterwards before you can apply paint. You will need to sand it before painting to create a key for the primer, too. Then there is the matter of protection. It is extremely corrosive and will harm your skin if it comes into contact with it. It also cuts through rubber and latex gloves, so you will need something heavy-duty and non-porous. Also, the fumes are toxic, so breathing apparatus is a must.

STRIPPING RUST

Rust is oxidized steel and must be cut out and removed, otherwise it will spread. Whether you weld in a repair section, or replace the entire panel, all surfaces should be absolutely free of rust before any material is applied. No matter how small the oxidized area is, it will grow, bubble up and destroy your paint job.

Generally speaking, surface rust is eminently treatable, and as long as the metal has no holes, and is a bright orange colour rather than deep brown, you will not have to resort to tearing it out completely – though this is the only way you can guarantee that it doesn't reappear. That said, it is time-consuming and costly.

Chemical treatments fall into two groups: acid and acid-free solutions. Acid-based solutions, which can be a liquid, gel or spray, dissolve the oxidized metal. Some products also leave a zinc phosphate coating that temporarily protects the naked metal from new rust forming. Acid-free solutions use a chemical reaction called chelating to remove the errant corrosion. This can be in the form of a solution, but there are conversion products designed to salvage some of the rusty metal rather than just dissolve it. These tend to be pulsed electrolytic kits that use a small electric current in an alkaline solution to transform corroded areas back into sound metal, bringing rust to bright metal in around twelve hours.

Acid products work more quickly and heat can be added as a catalyst, speeding up the process. However, acid baths tend to be very aggressive and can actually eat away at the metal itself, making it thinner if left to soak for too long. Conversely, non-acidic baths take longer to remove rust, but do not require such careful monitoring

Now all you have to do is simply deal with the metal underneath.

CHAPTER FOUR

DENT REPAIR AND RUST PROOFING

This chapter answers the following questions:

• How do I repair minor dents and dings?
• What is the best way to use body filler, and should I use it at all?
• How do I repair a panel using lead loading?
• What is the best way to achieve a pebble-smooth surface to apply my filler to?

Rust kills cars, and you must mitigate against it reappearing at every step of the way. Here, you will be able to learn the best ways to stop it spreading onto your panels underneath your fresh paint, as well as making sure that every surface is smooth and dent-free.

PANEL REPAIR BASICS

Now you should be in a position to either see the metalwork that will underpin your paint job or have a good idea what condition it is in. Chances are, there will be some problems – dents, scratches and rust are common, but eminently fixable. But before making

You would be surprised by how well metalwork responds to panel beating.

Sometimes you have to admit defeat and source a new part.

Cast your net widely when sourcing panels. Countries that have very little rain are a good option.

any sort of adjustments or removals, ensure your door hinges are in good condition. Every panel from the wing backwards lines up with the door, an area prone to sagging due to worn hinges, especially on coupé and convertibles, which tend to have longer doors than their saloon counterparts. Once you are absolutely sure everything is in the best possible condition, begin removing errant panels.

Faced with a particularly disastrous panel – bitten by rust or stuffed with body filler, for example – it is far more cost and time effective to simply replace the panel, providing they are available for your car. To check what is available for your car, take your chassis number (not just the registration number – sometimes there are small differences in sheet metal from model to model that aren't pulled up from a registration number-based parts' enquiry) to the dealer and have them search on your behalf. Original equipment manufacturer (OEM) panels are expensive, but generally offer the best fit and highest quality.

If your car is particularly unusual or was manufactured by a carmaker that no longer exists, an internet search will reveal the best places to buy new repair panels. But be careful – nothing will fit your car as well as the original parts, or parts made by the manufacturer using its factory dies. A second-hand original wing, for example, will usually give far fewer fitment and alignment problems than a new part made from a pattern. If you search extensively enough, and recruit members of owners' clubs and enthusiast groups, you may find an older part costs less as well. It is also worth casting your net across the Atlantic. There are thousands of scrap yards to choose from in American 'dry' states (where there is little rain, like Nevada and Arizona). Many will offer international postage, or at least be able to post to port areas where several companies that specialize in European shipping will be able to float it across the Atlantic and deal with the customs and excise charges on your behalf. Remember not to worry about matching colour, either – provided you follow the same steps as you do preparing the rest of your car, it will be unnoticeable once the vehicle has been painted.

Provided you are careful and you can reach both sides, you can reshape metal with a hammer.

That said, there is more value attached to a car fitted with its original parts. Given enough time and money, anything can be repaired, and sometimes even severe maladies can be corrected with surprisingly little time. We will deal with basic sheet metal repair here, but you should remember that many of these techniques require a lot of practice to get right, and years to master, so it is worth getting hold of an old scrap panel to practice on. Better still, attend a metalwork restoration course from an organization like Contour Autocraft – it offers courses for every element of fabrication and repair.

HAMMER AND DOLLY

The most basic method of fixing dents is to gently tap bent metal until it returns to the factory shape. This is only possible if you can reach both sides of the metal, because you need to use a hammer on the raised section of the dent, and a dolly on the backside (usually the paint side) that matches the contour of the panel. This technique is called hammer-on-dolly. If you have concerns about marking the metal, you can use a spoon instead of a hammer – it looks like a flat, narrow trowel and because the tool is far wider, leaves shallower indentations on the surface below.

Hammer-off-dolly panel beating minimizes the risk of stretching metal.

Use heat to restore a panel's surface radius.

It can also be used to prize up larger dents, and take out small high spots in curved sections.

You can also use the hammer-off-dolly method, a technique that minimizes the risk of stretching metal over the dolly. In this instance, the taps you make with the hammer land around the edge of the dent but the dolly is below the centre of the dent. So you tap the high spots with the hammer, and push up on the low spots with the dolly, which eventually straightens out the metal.

HEAT SHRINKING

Older cars built with thicker metal can be repaired using heat. Dents or metal that has become bowed can be popped back into place by heating a penny-sized section of the dent with an acetylene torch to around 1,200°C (2,190°F), then cooling it rapidly with a wet rag. You can also use a portable propane torch, but remember it needs to be upright, so you may need to remove the panel to heat it.

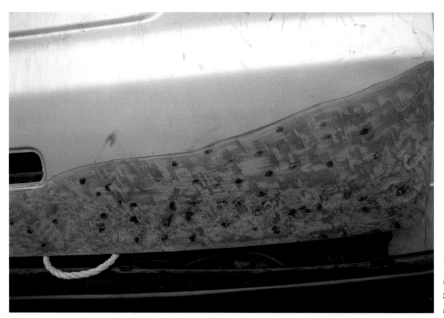

Your panel will look like this after heat shrinking – straight but burned.

Lead Loading

This is an old-fashioned way to repair your panel; instead of a filler product, you replace metal with metal. There are also lead-free body solder alternatives, but this guide covers the original method. You will need heat and flame-proof welders' gloves for this, as well as breathing apparatus and eye protection due to lead's toxicity.

Lead loading flux.

What this does is partially realign the steel molecules to their original shape, as well as hardening the material – but beware. As with all metalworking reshaping techniques, there is a possibility you can do more harm than good. This technique can warp thinner metal, as you would find on a roof, bonnet or boot lid. Modern cars are often built using a lighter gauge steel as well, so it should be reserved for thick-metal classics. Speak to your owners' club to see if any members have had success with the heat-shrinking method.

Also, this technique is only really appropriate for indentations, as opposed to creases. If you heat a creased area, it will harden it, making repairs with a hammer and dolly more difficult.

FLUX

Brush on the solder paste from your kit over the whole area, which should be cleaned and sanded to shiny metal. This both cleans the metal chemically and lays down a thin layer of lead.

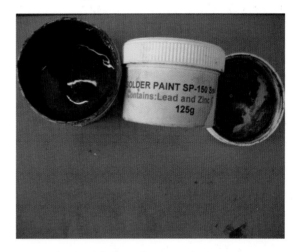

Lead loading solder paste.

SOLDER PASTE

Heat the solder paste until it melts across the surface of the panel, then wipe with a clean cloth. This should remove the paste and leave you with a thin layer of lead. Once cooled, wash and dry the area to get rid of acid residue.

LEAD

Focus heat onto the lead stick, but try and keep the panel warm at the same time. When the stick begins to melt push it hard onto the panel with a twist, which should leave small balls of lead on the surface of the metal.

Lead loading lead.

PADDLE

Dip your wooden paddle in tallow to keep it lubricated, then heat the balls until they become malleable. Push the lead into errant bodywork with the paddle. If you find yourself running out of lead, you can move lead deposits around the work area by heating them, then using the paddle to push the material into your repair section.

SANDING

Use a body file to smooth out the lead (power tools will cause lead dust, which is a major health hazard), but be careful as it will groove your body panel if you are too enthusiastic. Getting the panel perfectly smooth will most likely require a few lead applications, but remember that lead shavings removed from the panel can be re-used. Once you feel as if you have done all you can with a body file, start with 40-grit production paper, followed by 80 grit, 120 grit, then finish with 180 grit. Make sure your breathing apparatus is functioning as it should, as this stage is the most hazardous. It should be smooth enough for priming at this stage.

FINISHING

Once your lead is shaped, wash the area to remove all the flux (a material that encourages rust) then use a solvent cleaner to remove any tallow before priming.

Lead loading paddle.

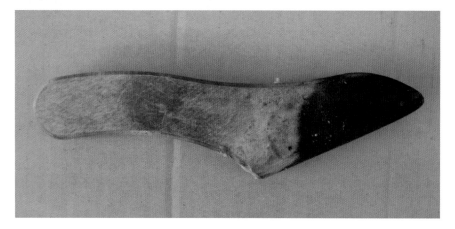

After lead loading.

BODY FILLER

Filler can be a dirty word when it comes to body-work, thanks largely to the legacy of unscrupulous body shops that have rebuilt entire structural sections with it. However, used sparingly – no more than 3mm – and correctly – applied after all repairs, and to naked metal keyed with 36-grit production paper – you can build a pebble-smooth base on which to paint your primer. Remember, you will have an opportunity to make additional corrections after the car has been primed, but this is your only time to attack it with a durable product, as thicker fillers can only be applied to bare metal or they will not adhere properly.

Unless you have supreme metalwork skills, any dent repairs using the techniques above will require an additional skim of filler for a perfectly smooth surface. Use a steel ruler (aluminium rulers can kink) at an angle allowing it to bend to the shape of the panel and show the position of the imperfection (you should be able to see a gap between the ruler and the panel), then mark up your repair area with a pen. Filler does not adhere well to graphite, which is what you'd leave if you used a pencil.

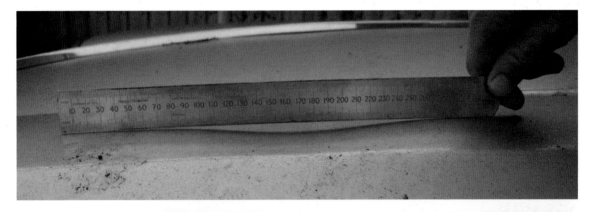

Steel rulers are an unlikely and extremely useful tool for measuring dent repairs.

Filler should be mixed at a ratio of 90 per cent filler and 10 per cent hardener.

It will turn a beige colour when cured.

Mix the filler to a 90 per cent filler/10 per cent hardener ratio, making sure the finished product is one uniform colour. If you can see strands of hardener colour, you need to keep mixing. Now apply sparingly with a clean, flexible plastic spatula – remember, most of the filler will be removed. Apply some pressure when you apply the mix, and make sure it fills all dented areas, but be careful not to overwork the material. If you are still manipulating the material, you can create pinholes and bubbles more easily. Before the mix has cured, you can use the ruler again to remove excess. Depending on the ambient temperature and filler/hardener ratio, it takes around two minutes to begin hardening.

The material should be dry and ready to sand after a maximum of thirty minutes depending on the ambient temperature, but try and leave for longer if you are working in the cold. Better still, use a heat lamp to help the process along. Hardened filler should feel absolutely dry and hard, without any tackiness. Also, if the production paper clogs, the filler is not yet ready to sand. That said, if left, say, overnight, it will become extremely difficult to sand.

Initially, make a few passes over the filled area with a sanding block to check if the panel requires additional product. Areas with a dark colouration indicate low spots, and will require more filler to create an even, smooth surface. You may need to apply several coats of filler, so ensure you remove all filler dust from the surface before you begin application. You should also ensure you have appropriate breathing apparatus, because the dust is extremely toxic.

Now use 80-grit paper to remove the excess, and keep checking with your ruler. You can use a sanding block, but regularly checking against the ruler will give a far better feel for the shape of the panel. Check your production paper regularly too. When it loses its colour, it will no longer sand, so you should replace accordingly. Also check the paper itself has not clogged. You can tell when this has happened because you will only be able to see filler dust on the abrasive side.

Make sure you have the correct breathing apparatus when you come to sand filler.

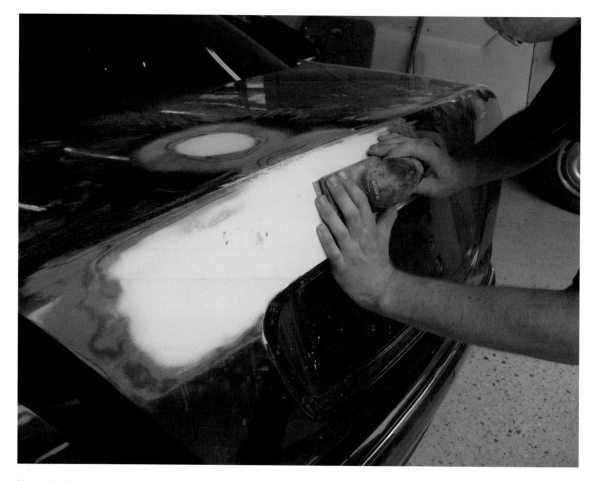

You will find that most of the filler is removed once.

STOPPERS AND PUTTY

Filler alone may not leave a smooth enough surface to paint over. There will be pinholes and scratches from the production paper, which will show through your top coat of paint. After waiting for the filler to fully cure, you can finish off repairs with a number of additional stoppers and putties. Lightweight polyester finishing fillers, like U-Pol's Fantastic, are designed as an additional topcoat for this very reason. They do not have the body to fill deeper holes, but because they sand very easily, they can mask scratches. On top of that, there are self-levelling stoppers that can be skimmed on and left to cure with minimal – if any – sanding afterwards. You can also apply some finishing fillers after you have primed your car provided that you have keyed the panel thoroughly.

A more traditional material is knifing putty, which can be applied by a flat, plastic spatula (the same sort you'd use to fill). Buy a tube of it – it is less susceptible to drying out than a tin – and spread sparingly over your filled panel. It is a cellulose material and will sink, so make sure deep scratches are properly filled beforehand.

To add a final key without deep scratches, use a fine production paper such as 240 grit. Use the paper dry at first, then wet to achieve the smoothest surface. Remember that filler absorbs water, so after sanding knifing putty, no primers should be applied after at least twenty-four hours. After the surface is dry, there will be a chance that bare metal areas will have picked up surface rust. Go over the metal areas with a medium paper like 100 grit to remove it before priming.

Knifing putty.

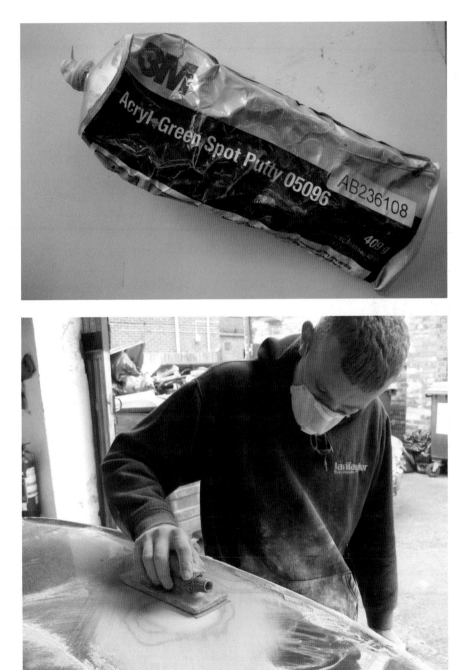

Use a fine production paper like 240 grit before priming.

FURTHER READING

This chapter is designed as a very basic guide to panel repairs, and barely scratches the surface of metalwork manipulation techniques, welding methods and panel fabrication. There are several guides that focus on these topics – each a large book's worth in itself.

CHAPTER FIVE

PAINTING TECHNIQUE

This chapter answers the following questions:

- How do I master my spray gun (what to practise with, how to get the best from your spray gun and compressor combination, how to lay the perfect coat, manoeuvring the gun, timings, staging and how to paint different materials)?
- How do I mix the perfect paint (combining thinners and paint successfully?)
- Is there anything I can do to get the most from my ability (the best conditions you can paint in and why they're important)?

Now you should have a fully sealed, fully repaired car body ready to paint. But before you dive into the job of priming and painting, you should take plenty of time to master all of your painting equipment.

AIR QUALITY

The importance of a good-quality air supply was covered in Chapter 2, but it cannot be emphasized enough because of the degree to which it can improve or damage your paint job. Make sure you have your compressor, air cooler and filtration in place – regardless of how well you mix your paint, how well you have prepared your car body and how well you have set up your work space, a poor air supply can ruin a paint finish.

An air compressor with dry air system.

Different spray guns have their own pros and cons.

SPRAY GUN BASICS

Rule one for novice painters is buy the best possible gun. While there are many available second-hand, you should always try to buy new equipment – there are so many ways that an old gun can be neglected and damaged, which will have a major impact on the quality of your paint finish. It really is not worth the bother. Using a poor gun could also affect the paint itself – if the gun is badly built, it may not be able to atomize the liquid at a paint manufacturer's recommended ratio of colour, thinner and hardener. Budget for around £200, which sounds like a lot, but if you maintain it properly, it will last indefinitely.

There are two main designs you should consider for painting your car – gravity-fed guns (where the paint cup is on the top) and suction-fed guns (where the paint cup is on the bottom). The advantage of a suction-fed gun is that it holds more material, but gravity-fed models are lighter and more manoeuvrable. Size varies – mini-jet guns are small, hold less material and work at a lower pressure, so are ideal for localized repairs, but not for painting a whole car. Standard-sized guns are good all-rounders, and are able to tackle localized repairs as well as full repairs, regardless of the size of your vehicle.

The two guns you should consider: gravity fed and suction fed.

TYPES OF PAINT GUNS

There are two main types of paint gun on the market: air paint guns and airless paint guns. While they do not require a compressor, airless guns will spray on too much paint too quickly, and are not suitable for automotive applications. Air paint guns can be further subcategorized into standard and high-volume low-pressure (HVLP) units.

A standard non-HVLP paint gun.

STANDARD GUNS

Droplets of paint form when mixed with compressed air. When they leave the nozzle, they are atomized and applied to a surface to form a smooth, even coating. Because the paint needs to be atomized through the nozzle before it lands on your car, it must be thinned as per the paint manufacturer's recommendations.

HVLP GUNS

Like a standard gun, HVLP units transform paint into extremely small droplets, and then spread them onto the surface. The difference is the air: in a standard gun, the atomization process is achieved with air pressure; in an HVLP unit, it is achieved with air volume. Using low-pressure compressed air (around 10psi at the head), an HVLP gun gets up to 65 per cent of the paint onto the surface. This transfer rate is called transfer efficiency (TE). A standard gun will have a TE of around 25 per cent, so the advantages when it comes to overspray (paint that does not reach the surface) and material costs (paint and thinners) are huge. These

High-volume low-pressure (HVLP) guns will reduce your paint spend.

OTHER CONSIDERATIONS

If you use the wrong paint or mix it incorrectly, it can be too thick for the gun and clog the nozzle, as will paint that is left to dry in the gun. This will affect the spray pattern and drastically reduce the quality of your finish. Make sure your gun is easy to clean and service. Look out for a reversible tip feature – by turning around the nozzle, you can use your compressed air supply to fire dried or thick paint out of the nozzle. Also, consider the availability of spare parts, so chose an established brand like Devilbiss, Sata and Iawata.

The paint gun rating sticker/stamp will tell you the cfm requirement.

guns do require the paint to be thinner, but the savings you make using this kind of equipment means the increased cost is negligible. These are the better of the two, and what you should opt for if your budget allows (they tend to be slightly more expensive).

GUN RATING

Every gun is rated by the amount of air (measured in cfm) it delivers at a certain psi. In practical terms, this means you need to make sure your compressor is appropriately rated to your gun. So your compressor must be able to produce the volume of air at that pressure consistently while you use the paint gun. As a rule, you should ensure your compressor is rated slightly above the gun's requirements – 1.5 times the cfm will suffice.

A paint gun that has been taken apart.

A TOUR OF YOUR SPRAY GUN

There are three variables that affect the spray pattern of your gun:

• Air flow valve. This is a screw or knob on the back of the gun that adjusts the amount of air pressure fed into the gun.

• Material control valve. This is usually adjusted by the knob above or below the air flow valve, and allows you to adjust the amount of paint that leaves your gun.

• Needle adjuster. This adjusts the amount of travel your paint gun trigger has. You tend to leave it so the trigger has full travel if you are painting a large panel, but may wish to reduce the paint flow for smaller parts.

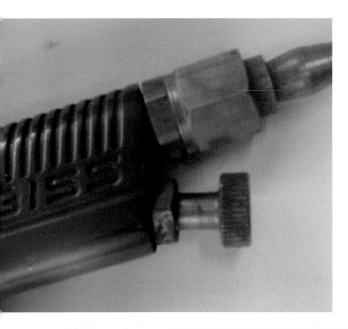

Air flow valve.

Material flow valve (top) and needle adjuster (bottom).

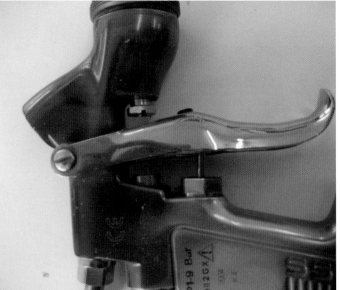

Trigger.

PAINT GUN TRIGGER

Each spray gun has two stages. Pull it lightly and it will open the valve but no paint will come out. Pull beyond the first stage of resistance and the paint needle is pulled out of the paint nozzle, and your material will come out of the gun.

PICKUP TUBE

This allows the paint to reach the nozzle from the pot. As the amount of paint in the pot reduces, you will have to loosen the nut at the top to adjust the angle of the paint. This is something you should not do while you are in the middle of your paint job. If you are painting the top side of the car you should set it forwards so you avoid having to refill the pot when it is already half full. Conversely, if you want to shoot the underside, turn it backwards to match the angle you will be painting at.

PAINT FILTER

Always use a filter on your gun. Hard paint from the edge of the tin can fall into the pot and end up as unsightly splats on your finished surface. You can leave it in place and wash it along with the rest of the gun. As long as the gun is used and cleaned regularly, the filter can last for as long as the lifetime of the gun.

Pickup tube.

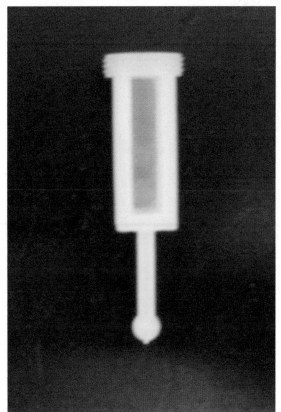

Paint filter.

Local legislation states that paint needs to be kept in a fireproof cabinet.

PAINT SAFETY

As we have mentioned throughout this book, paint is extremely flammable and extremely toxic, and must be stored in a fireproof cabinet. Also, some local councils impose a limit on the amount of paint and associated materials you are allowed to keep in your home or garage, and you must check their guidelines before you buy any of your materials, as some legislation may make it unfeasible to undertake the job at home.

HOW TO MIX PAINT PROPERLY

Before you begin to mix the paint, make sure you are using a paint system – regardless of how many stages – from the same manufacturer. If you mix and match from different companies, you risk durability, bonding and adhesion problems. Also, if you do have problems with the finished result, no single company will stand by their guarantee because it could be a matter of chemical compatibility. As a precautionary measure, read both the instructions on your paint gun and your air compressor, then take them to your paint supplier so they can sell you the best material for your equipment.

Paint materials tend to be transported as concentrates to avoid any of the solid materials like pigments settling, then whoever is spraying it can dilute them depending on the conditions in which they are using

Paint and thinners must always be part of the same system.

vary. The most common systems from mainstream manufacturers like ICI and Max Meyer tend to be comprised of three different ingredients: solid colour, hardener and thinner. While the colour component tends to be standard, hardeners and thinners are available to suit different temperatures and seasons, and come in slow, medium and fast-drying variations. Speak to your paint supplier to see which will be the most appropriate.

When it comes to mixing ratios, you should stick to the manufacturer's recommendation and use a clean container, preferably a disposable painter's cup, which looks like an ordinary water cup but has measurements printed on the side. If they are unavailable, you can use a calibrated mixing stick, which should also be available from your supplier – they have numbers or marks inscribed on them that tell you how much of each material needs to be poured. Stir each individual liquid using a new, clean mixing stirrer (not a dirty screwdriver) every time you paint because the materials may have settled, so you will need to drag the sludge from the bottom of the tin up to the surface so it mixes as the manufacturer intended.

To remove any contamination, you should strain each material before you pour them into your container, and allow a few moments from tipping in the material to tipping in the next ingredient for it to pass through the strainer and settle. Mix your materials in the cup according to the ratios specified, then give it another, thorough stir. When you come to pour it in the spray gun cup, give it a shake before painting. Never pour each individual component into the paint cup – it will not mix properly and will clog your paint filter because all the thick material will sink to the bottom. Now put the lid back on all the materials to avoid it hardening, drying, evaporating or spilling.

HOW TO MASTER A PAINT GUN

Before painting your car, you should master your gun on a scrap panel.

BEFORE YOU PAINT

Check every nut, bolt and seal on the gun for a tight fit, and even if you bought a brand-new gun, ensure

Mitigate unwanted particles entering your paint job with a filter.

the product, so they are suitable for spraying. Also, paint that uses a hardener cannot be stored as a ready-to-spray mix because the hardening process begins as soon as it is applied. This is worth remembering if you plan on mixing large batches of paint – this should be avoided, not only because the paint will be unusable, but because you will have to get rid of it afterwards. This will mean going to a specialist chemical disposal centre, or paying your local paint shop or distributor to do the job for you. Local authorities do not look kindly on storage of chemical waste at home. If you mistakenly mix up too much paint, you may be able to dispose of it for a small fee via your local body shop, though they have no obligation to help you.

The most commonly used automotive paint will be a two-pack system, but the ingredients that make them up – and the amount of ingredients – can

Ready for painting.

One last check before the job begins.

the air feed hose and union are not leaking. Make sure there are no naked flames, either – that includes candles, cigarettes and some space heaters.

Using an HVLP unit, set the pressure to 29psi. Most modern guns will have a digital readout or compressed air control gauge, but if your gun is not equipped with one, you can adjust your inlet pressure in-line moisture trap to 9psi higher than 29psi for every 10m (33ft) of air hose. This compensates for any drop of pressure as air passes through the hose to your gun.

THE FAN

What you are trying to achieve is paint evenly distributed inside your spray fan. To this end, you need to practise adjusting the air valve on your paint gun. Some guns have their own fan control. Experiment on a piece of paper – you will find that with the air valve closed, the paint will tend to build up heavily towards the centre of the spray fan, which will mean a streaky finish to your panel. As you open the valve, the paint will distribute itself more widely across the fan. But if you open it too widely, too much paint will pass through, which will cause runs. For guns with a fan control dial, turn it the left for a flat spray and turn to the right for a round spray.

THE PRESSURE

Once you have mastered the correct spray fan, you need to work out what pressure you are comfortable spraying with, which relates to the speed with which you sweep across the panel. You should aim for the lowest air pressure that still gives you a good rate of application and atomization (when the paint becomes a fine spray). If the pressure is too high, you will lose a lot of paint to overspray; and if the pressure is too low, the finish will have an orange peel effect, and sag.

If you are using a conventional siphon gun, try setting the pressure to around 50psi and spraying across a piece of paper. Reduce the pressure in 5psi increments until the rate of coverage and droplet size is insufficient. Now bump up the pressure to the lowest possible pressure that offers a rate of coverage you are comfortable painting at and you will arrive at the ideal rate.

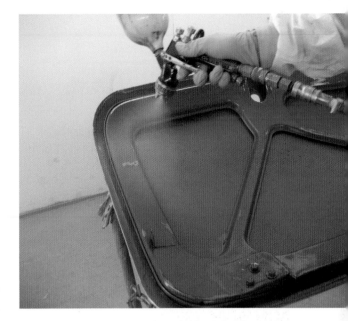

Fine tune your fan for the best finish.

The speed you paint relates to the pressure you paint at faster equals higher.

Keeping a constant distance from the panel is essential.

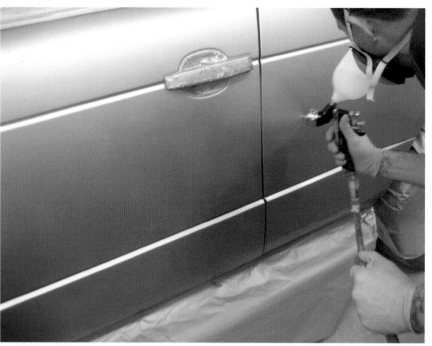

Always spray beyond the panel.

THE DISTANCE

Keep the gun between 15 and 20cm (6 and 8in) from the panel and make sure the gun is at right angles from the panel at all times – this will require you to move your hand as the shape of the panel changes so the paint is not heavy at one end of the spray fan.

THE SPEED

Move the gun in a straight line at a constant speed across the panel and do not stop at the edge of the panel – move the gun as if you were spraying for around 7cm (3in) beyond the panel so there is no heavy paint build-up at each end. When you approach the edge of the panel, release the trigger so the paint flow stops but the air flow does not, then re-introduce the paint as you pass back onto the panel.

PASS BY PASS

You should overlap each pass by around 50 per cent. The centre of the spray pattern should be aimed at the edge of the previous stroke. If you need to overlap more there is a chance your fan pattern needs adjusting because there is too much paint at the centre. If you find you need to overlap more than that the chances are you have too much paint in the centre of the fan. The paint gun should land on the panel with a very slight orange peel effect, then settle into a smooth finish.

Each pass should overlap.

PAINT GUN AND FINISH TROUBLESHOOTING

If the orange peel finish remains, there is not enough paint coming through the gun. Increase the paint flow or pressure. If the paint lands on the panel as a flat, smooth sheet, but begins to drip or sag, reduce the paint flow and pressure.

LEAKING TIP

If the gun leaks fluid from the tip, something has got between the fluid tip and needle, which prevents a proper seal. Remove and clean the needle and nozzle, or use a new nozzle set. If it leaks from the needle, the sealing is damaged and should be replaced.

DEFECTIVE SPRAY PATTERN

If your spray pattern is the shape of a sickle, your air circuit is clogged somewhere. Soak the nozzle in thinner and use the manufacturer's recommended cleaning needle.

If the spray patter is oval or drop-like, you have a dirty nozzle or compromised air supply. Try turning the nozzle through 180 degrees. If it persists, clean the nozzle and check your air circuit's filtration system.

FLUTTERING SPRAY

If the paint fails to come out in an even mist, there are three things to check: you may have too little material in the cup, the nozzle is not mounted tightly enough, or the needle sealing is dirty or damaged.

BUBBLING PAINT

If your material bubbles in the paint cup, you have an air leak that is flowing through the liquid. Check all screws are tightened and that the nozzle is clean. If the problem persists, you may need to check the nozzle for wear or damage.

Keep an eye out for leaks.

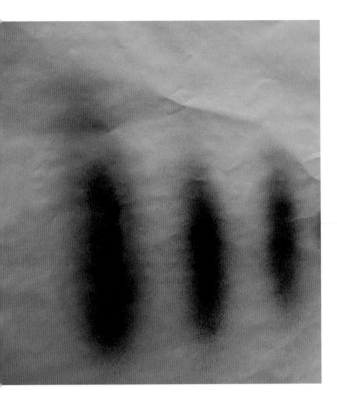

If your spray pattern starts wavering, it is time to stop painting.

Bubbling paint means air leaks.

ALWAYS USE THE GUN MANUFACTURER'S OFFICIAL PARTS

To make sure that your gun's warranty remains intact and that your equipment is operating as best it possibly can, always use the original manufacturer's parts. All major companies will carry every conceivable spare part.

MAKE LIFE EASIER WITH LIGHTING

The more you can see, the more you see what is going right or wrong. Install as much lighting in your workspace as you possibly can, and remember that side lighting is as important as overhead lighting. This is not so much to illuminate the area, as to reflect the wet paint, allowing you to examine its texture as you spray it on.

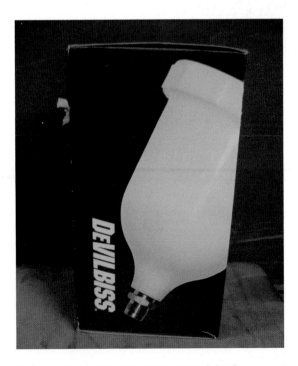

As you would with your car, use original equipment manufacturer parts.

The more you light you have, the more you will know how your paint is being applied.

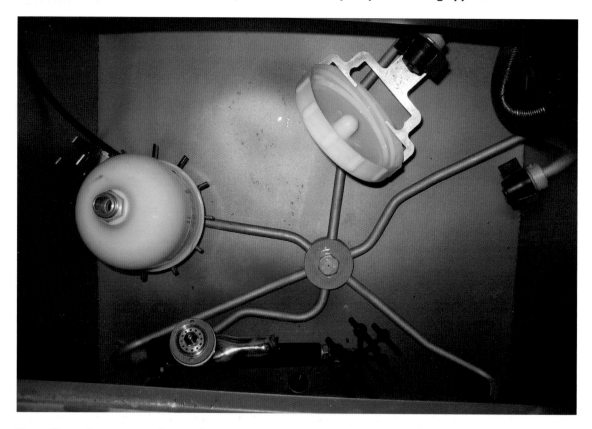

You will need your gun to be spotless before you begin painting.

Use thinners to flush your paint gun.

THE IDEAL CONDITIONS FOR PAINTING

As covered in Chapter 2, ideal temperatures to paint in are between 15 and 20°C (60 and 68°F). If your workspace is much colder, moisture will find its way into the paint. When the paint dries, moisture will remain beneath it and bubble up causing microblistering. If your workspace is too warm, the paint will not be able to flow properly as it dries too quickly, which will give the finish an orange peel effect.

CLEANING AND MAINTENANCE

You will need to clean your gun between every painting session to avoid any material hardening and clogging your equipment. There are specialist paint gun washing machines available, and they do an excellent job of purging errant paint, but at anything from £1,500 this is a very costly commodity. You may wish to contact your local paint shop and, provided it is compatible with your gun, ask if you can rent their machine. Alternatively, service it yourself, but be

extremely careful as you will be dealing with delicate parts. When dismantling the gun, you should not have to use any great force. Consult the literature that comes with the gun for any specific tools or equipment you might need for the job.

With it disconnected from the air supply and all hoses removed, flush the gun through thoroughly with thinners. Now clean the air nozzle with a paint brush – avoid submerging it in cleaner or thinners because it may damage rubber or neoprene O-rings.

If you encounter any clogged parts (like the nozzle, for example), do not use pointed, sharp-edged or abrasive tools because it will affect the spray pattern and the gun's adjustability. Soak it in thinners instead, and follow the manufacturer's guidelines for the length of time it can be soaked – leaving it in a thinners' bath for too long can also damage some components.

When it comes to reassembly, very slightly oil all the moving parts, and check that all seals and rubber O-rings are in good condition and fit tightly against every surface.

Now you are ready to mask your car and start thinking about priming.

CHAPTER SIX

MASKING

This chapter answers the following questions:

• How do I mask my car?
• What materials can I use?
• Do I need to remove everything to mask properly?
• Do I need to remove my engine?

It seems like a straightforward job, but there are lots of considerations to take into account when you prepare your car for paintwork, including choosing the correct materials, and shortcuts you can make that will make the job easier.

MASKING

After you have made any necessary adjustments and repairs to your bodywork, you will need to mask the car before you can put the shell or panels in primer. However neat you are, overspray will land on body panels or trim, and if you want a top-quality paint job, you will have to remove it. It is infinitely more time-efficient to properly mask your car in the first place than to go over it once you have painted, and in most cases you will find removal of trim pieces and parts like headlights and bumpers far easier than masking over them.

Ideally, you will be working with a bare shell that has had everything removed, but for localized repairs this may not be required or necessary (but

A car masked and ready for the booth.

remember that it is always best to paint the entire car or else you risk poorly matched colours). That said, masking anything other than a bare shell is an extremely time-consuming task, and you will need to be precise and meticulous. Whatever you chose and whatever painting job you plan to undertake, you should familiarize yourself with the materials before you get to work.

MASKING TAPE

Only ever use masking tape designed for the job, which will be available from an automotive paint store. There is a huge difference between automotive masking tape and household products. Tape designed for automotive refinishing will stand up to the strong solvents you find in car paint – if you use domestic products, they may seep through or under the tape and damage the finish underneath. The adhesives used differ too – on a tailor-made tape, you should be able to remove it easily, whereas domestic products may require a solvent to lift the residue, which could also damage your paint.

Automotive refinishing tape is available is various widths for various jobs – around seven in total, from $^1/_8$in to 2in. The most useful size is 1.5in as you can use it for securing paper and covering areas such as key lock holes and aerial apertures. A roll each of 1in, 1.5in and 2in should be more than enough to cover a DIY paint job. Use small tape to mask things that you cannot remove, and the wider sizes for surfaces not quite large enough to warrant masking paper.

To ensure a perfectly straight line between spraying areas, you may also wish to use plastic tape, like 3M's Fine Line. It is very manoeuvrable and will stick around curves without bending or ruffling. Apply it before any other tapes, then add a wider masking tape – that way you will not have to apply every piece of masking tape right up to the edge of the masked area. Whilst painting a car with some trim left on is not recommended, this product is useful for this purpose.

Fine Line tape is also very useful for applying stripes or graphics because, unlike masking tape, it has a coating on it to stop paint sticking to it, so when you peel it off it leaves a straight and fine line.

You must use masking tape designed for the job.

3M Fine Line is the industry leader.

Paint can stick to masking tape, so when you come to remove it, it can lift some of the paint with it. When laying out patterns, mask with tape and edge with Fine Line.

MASKING PAPER

While it may seem like a viable and cheap option, avoid using newspaper as it can let some paint absorb and seep through – instead buy some proper auto-

You can also use Fine Line to apply graphics and panels of different colour.

You will need a selection of masking papers.

motive masking paper. Widths range from 6in to 48in, though you will probably find 18in the most useful. Two rolls should be enough for a full paint job, but if you are undertaking a smaller repair and want to mask large sections like roofs or bonnets, you should buy wider paper. It is also available with masking tape already applied to one edge for ease of use.

Professional painters may use a masking paper rack that has various widths on it, but you can buy smaller hand-held dispensers, re-purpose a kitchen roll dispenser or just make your own up. If you can, mount it solidly on a nearby work surface by clamping if down or screwing it into a piece of old wood so you can pull the paper if freely.

NOW BEGIN MASKING

For the best results, you should not spray a vehicle piecemeal, and each coat of primer or paint should be applied in one session onto a fully masked car. But if you are conducting a localized repair, you should mask everywhere but the immediate area you intend to paint. Even if you are painting the driver's side of the car, overspray may settle onto the trim of the passenger side. The best way to avoid this is by applying a large plastic sheet over the area, then securing it with masking tape. You can buy this from a paint supplier, but it comes in 200m rolls, which may be too much if you are considering painting just one car. Alternatively, they are available from large supermarkets or DIY shops and are incredibly cheap.

WINDOWS

To avoid paint build-up around masked edges and overspray on rubber mouldings, you should always remove the screen and associated seals. Failing that, use a specialist weather strip masking tool. It uses lengths of plastic cord that lift the seal, allowing you to spray under it, not just up to the edge of it, which stops you having

RIGHT: *You do not need to buy a professional product – think creatively about what you can use.*

A masked car.

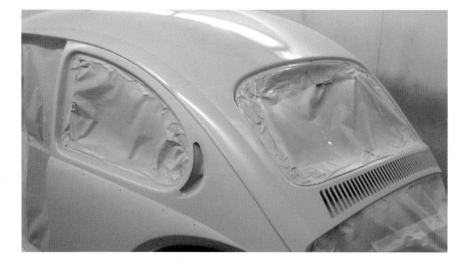

A couple of masked window apertures.

unsightly paint edge lines. Though without removing the window completely, you will not be able to see if the metal underneath is in good condition – most window apertures on older cars are a rust hot-spot.

If you decide to use this method, apply plastic tape around the edges of the rubber – making sure there are no ruffles in the tape – then apply wider masking tape anywhere along the plastic tape to fasten your masking tape into place.

Regardless of whether you removed the windows or not, you will need to mask the aperture, so protect your glass or interior. Providing you have bought masking paper designed for the job, you should only need to use a single sheet for it, though larger cars may need more material to properly plug the gap. If you are painting a bare shell, apply paper from inside the car to ensure that you paint the edge that your rubber seal mounts to. This will protect it from rust.

Make sure any masking paper used in large sections is pulled relatively taut by folding it. Put one hand behind any baggy sections, and use the other to grip and fold it, then fasten the fold with masking paper making sure any crease is sealed shut. Bigger paper bulges can get blown around by compressed air from a paint gun, and if they are covered in lots of wet paint or primer, they may tear. This is worth remembering as a general rule, too – any gaps or folds in the masking paper should always be sealed shut, otherwise the compressed air from your gun will pull them open.

DOOR HANDLES AND LOCK APERTURES

Even stripped cars will have window-winder mechanisms or motors hiding behind the apertures left by a handle, so make sure these are masked. To avoid any paint edge lines, use strips of overlapped masking tape to seal the area shut from the inside of the door or boot – masking paper will probably be too awkward to work with as there will usually be two skins to a door panel and the inner will give limited access to the outer.

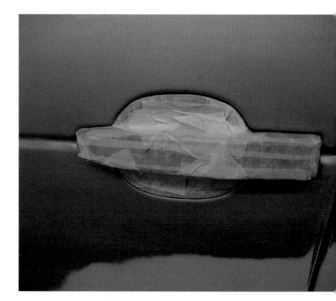

Mask door handles and lock apertures from behind.

DOOR JAMBS

This will be covered in more detail later, but to give your car the best possible finish you should spray the edges of your panels and any jambs (sections where panels are secured to the monocoque or body shell) individually, then once the primer or paint has dried, close the doors and mask the gaps to avoid over-spray, which you will have to sand off. If you leave the doors on instead of removing them and spraying them separately (the latter is recommended), apply some thick, 2in tape with the sticky side facing out to the bottom of the door, and the same to the jamb, when you close the door you can stick both bits of tape to each other and seal the gap.

There are also specialist products available like 3M's Soft Edge, which is like draft-excluding foam. Stick it on the door edge, close the door and it fills the gap. This avoids masking tape or paper flicking onto freshly-applied paint.

A freshly painted door jamb.

ENGINES

Removing engines is a time-consuming procedure that often requires specialist tools like hoists, and while it is ideal to have a completely bare shell, you can get a great long-lasting finish and leave it installed (providing the engine bay is not suffering from rust). However, there are delicate electrical connections and mechanical components that could be damaged by overspray – even if you use the very best HVLP gun – so you need to tightly seal the entire engine bay. Be aware that once it is masked, you will not be able to run the car, as the engine will get too hot and cause the paper to ignite.

As with indicator or fuel-filler cap holes, the easiest way to seal these areas is from the inside, so you can paint as much of the surface as possible. Most engine bays will have raised sections on the inside of the wings on which you can mount masking paper. You will find it easiest to mask each side individually, then tape both sections of paper together in the middle.

For the best results you should remove your engine, though it is not strictly necessary.

Engine removal allows you to mask from the inside and to get a comprehensive finish.

USE MASKING PAPER TO BLEND OLD PAINT WITH NEW

If you are touching in a panel that you have repainted on its own, you will need to blend in the old paint with the new. This technique is called feathering or melting, and you can use masking paper to avoid any obvious lines between your new coat and your old coat.

With all but a an inch of the old painted area masked, stick down some tape with paper as if you are masking the panel that you have just painted, then gently pull it back towards the masked area without folding the tape down, so the tape is curved. This gives you a gentle edge onto which you can spray, allowing the paint to bounce off the curve and create a softer blend between the panels.

Now empty all but around 5mm of paint in your gun, and add around 15mm of thinner, so the mixture is roughly 3:1. Remove just the curved masking paper, then spray the super-thinned paint onto the exposed area. The extra thinner will melt the old paint and allow a little colour onto the seam. There are also specialist fade-out thinners available that you can use neat – they come in either material form or in an aerosol. They eat into the old paint more aggressively, and prevent the extra-thinned paint rolling paint when you try and polish it at a later date.

Masking tape can also be used to melt in paint.

CHAPTER SEVEN

PRIMERS

This chapter answers the following questions:

• What type of primer should I use?
• How do I apply primer and paint to my car?
• How should I sand my car?
• How should I mask my car?

This is the last stop before painting and your last chance to iron out any remaining kinks or ruffles in your panels. There some important health and safety issues to consider at this stage, as well as additional ways to stop rust reappearing before your top coat. Now start your car's path to paint. You are almost there.

TOOLS AND MATERIALS FOR THIS CHAPTER

Primer This allows you to prepare the metal for paint.

Spray Gun You will need to spray on the primer, so make sure you use your dedicated primer gun or tip.

Masking Tape and Masking Paper Unless you have a completely bare shell, you will need to cover areas like the engine and dashboard so they do not get coated in primer or overspray, even if you are using an HVLP gun.

Sanding Blocks They are a useful tool as they do not follow local depressions in the panel like hand sanding, but make sure your block is flexible. Nearly every surface of every car, however square, will have some sort of curve in it.

Production Paper For block sanding, you will need anything from 0 to 220 grit depending on how aggressively you wish to prepare the car. You should opt for a few of self-adhesive papers to stop it falling off or folding under your sanding block.

Guide Coat It can be a specialist product, but most paint (providing it is part of your paint/primer system) will do as long it is in a contrasting colour to your primer.

Glazes and Stoppers You will need these to fix any low spots or small dings you missed in the initial stages of body preparation.

Breathing Apparatus You will be working with toxic paints and dust at this stage, so you need use a dust mask as a minimum.

Latex Gloves Just as it can affect your lungs, the toxic paint and dust can damage your skin.

PRIMER BASICS

With your paint gun technique mastered, your bodywork fully prepared and purged of rust, and your workspace primed for the job, you can begin to spray. However, before you start, you will need to choose a primer system for your masked car. You should try and make sure the system is from the same supplier as your paint system because other manufacturers' materials may not be compatible, which could compromise the finish. Like paint, the price variation between budget primer brands and mainstream manufacturers like ICI is around 50 per cent, but you should try and buy the best you can. Also consider the paint gun you will use. If your budget allows, buy one gun for priming and another for painting. If not, have a dedicated gun tip for use with primer and another for paint.

Try not to keep your car in primer for too long.

PRIMER SYSTEMS

Ordinarily, primer systems involve two stages. First, there is a very adhesive self-etch, on top of which you apply a high-build primer. The first coating is extremely adhesive and provides a barrier that prevents water ingress to your metalwork (and therefore corrosion), and the second is thicker, which allows you to cover very minor imperfections. The purpose of priming your car is to build a uniform substrate to which you can apply paint. Remember – like everything else that passes through your paint gun, primers should be strained before you use them. Also, factor in storage – once your car is primed, you won't be able to leave it outside, as many systems are porous and will allow water ingress, which will damage the metal underneath. But first you need to decide what type of primer fits your needs.

SELF-ETCHING PRIMER

Available as a high build or standard system, this should be used if you stripped your car back to bare steel, aluminium or glass reinforced plastic (GRP) and fibreglass. It is a mixture of phosphoric acid and zinc – the acid forces the zinc into the top of the metal, which keeps rust away and makes a formidable surface for putting another layer of material on top. You cannot use it if there is some pre-existing paint or filler on your panel as the acid will lift it and you would not be able to paint directly onto it without a layer of epoxy primer on top.

One coat of self-etching primer is plenty. Be sure to let your paint supplier know at what temperature you will be applying it because that affects the ratio of some two-part systems (some come with a hardener). Also remember that the chemicals in self-etching primers react with metal, so you will have to swap your metal spray gun cup with a plastic one. Use a modest paint gun tip, too – something between 1.4mm and 1.8mm to ensure it atomizes.

Self-etching primer is ideal for bare metal resprays.

When you come to apply it, make sure there is no dirt or oils on the panel by wiping it down with a degreasing panel wipe. Begin with a very fine mist coat because anything applied directly to naked metal – especially metal that has been filled – tends to run. Let it dry completely, then paint on your first proper coat. Once it is dry, it will need to be scuffed with a 400-grit abrasive to prepare it for the next layer of primer.

HIGH-BUILD PRIMER

High-build primer will always follow a layer of self-etching primer, and because it is a lot less volatile, it can be applied directly on top of filled, keyed paint-work – just as long as it is very clean. You can apply it directly to paint that has been sanded down with a mild abrasive like 240-grit production paper, but you will not be able to use it directly onto bare metal, as it will flake off.

As well as proving a stable substrate for your paint, it can be used to rectify minor body imperfections. That said, it should never be used as a substitute for proper filler/lead-loading/metalwork repairs, as it may shrink as it dries, making imperfections even more visible.

High-build primer will help rectify minor bodywork woes.

High-build primer is available in cellulose, two-pack and water-based (though the supply of cellulose materials has been restricted to classic car restoration and industrial use in the European Union). Because two-pack contains carcinogenic isocyanates, you will need to use a respiration kit and pay attention to safety requirements, but it is the better of the two because it has a hardener and will have a more chip-resistant finish. It tends to leave a thicker and smoother finish too, and is not as prone to sinkage as cellulose. Water-based products will be difficult to use if you are painting at home because you need specialist equipment to remove the water from the material. As a rule, it is best for amateurs to avoid all water-based paint products.

Like self-etching primer, it is available as a two-part system that includes a hardener, so you will need to make sure that both parts are mixed thoroughly. Using this system, you also need to tell your paint supplier when you intend to spray and what the temperature will be outside, as this will affect the ratios of the mixed material.

You should need no more than three coats. Find different colours to your self-etching primer and two different colours of high-build primer itself, so that when you come to cut it back, you will know if you have broken through to the layer below. This will stop you accidentally rubbing it back to bare metal with your abrasive and thereby compromising the self-etching coat.

You can use a metal cup to apply it, but ensure you use a gun tip between 1.4mm and 1.6mm. If you go beyond anything close to 2mm, it will not atomize properly and the gun will spit droplets onto the panel. It does not have to be completely dry before you apply the next layer – you can add another coat when it is tacky – but leave it for 48 hours before you key the surface with your 400-grit abrasive.

HEAT LAMPS

As mentioned previously, the ideal temperature at which to paint your car is between 15 and 20°C (60 and 68°F), and to achieve that in any other season than high summer, you will need to use heat lamps.

Paint in temperatures between 15 and 20°C (60 and 68°F).

When you spray primer or paint, make sure that all heating equipment is at least 1.5m (5ft) away from a freshly painted surface.

PRIMER COLOURS

Regardless of what primers you select, try and make sure that each layer of primer is a different colour, so that when you are using production paper to prepare the surface for paint, you will know if you have broken through to the next layer or not.

The colour of your primer will affect the surface colour.

While light grey primer is the most popular, there are several colours available to choose from. If your car's body has undergone extensive repairs, it may be better to use a darker colour, as you will find it easier to spot any imperfections in the panel (in much the same way that black paint shows more imperfections). Differing colours can also affect the final top coat's colour – add a light colour to a dark primer and you may have to use more top coat material to get to the same shade that you mixed on your work bench. If you are confident in your repair work, match the primer colour roughly to the colour you wish to paint.

NOW START SPRAYING PRIMER

You spray primer in much the same way as you would paint. You should take care not to build up excessive paint thickness at door edges, otherwise they may become prone to chipping because you will effectively be decreasing the size of the panel, increasing the chance of both of them meeting.

GUIDE COAT

The biggest advantage you can give yourself is to spray your primed car with guide coat. This is a thin mist of colour you can apply after priming the car. You sand off this layer so you can see any high or low spots, allowing for last minute corrections to be made before painting.

Spray the surface, sand it back using 240-grit production paper and the paint will remain in deep sanding scratches or small dents you may have missed when preparing the shell. Only once you have removed all of the guide coat from your panel – and the high points are level with the low points – will it be ready for paint.

There are specialist guide-coat dusts available, but because you will be sanding it all off you can use any old paint aerosols you have lying around in the garage.

SANDING

Now the work really begins. This is an absolutely critical stage, and one of the most time-consuming stages of the painting process. The professionals invest as much as 200 hours sanding, sometimes going over the entire car five times before they roll it into the spray booth. This is your last chance to get the panels as straight as possible before you apply paint, and fixing things at this point is far easier – and cheaper – than after you have applied your top coat. You will be dry sanding only (primers can be porous).

If, or rather when, you find defects at this stage, remember that they are entirely fixable. You will not be able to use body filler over primer, but you can use glazing putties (see Chapter 4) to make any necessary corrections, which should be all you need if you prepared the panel thoroughly. Self-levelling products will save you a tremendous amount of time and effort at this stage because they require little sanding, but apply sparingly so you remove as little of the surrounding primer as possible when sanding.

With your guide coat applied, pick a flat panel to begin with – something with as few creases as possible, like a bonnet, to build up your technique. If there are any creases or recesses in the panel, further divide up your work area by sanding within any edges (you can easily rub through to bare metal in as little as one sanding stroke on the shoulders of creases).

Begin with 240-grit production paper on a flexible sanding block (the longer and flatter the surface, the longer and flatter your block should be) and start slowly rubbing up and down. The harsher production paper gives the surface plenty of tooth to hold stoppers or putty.

Sanding a styling crease.

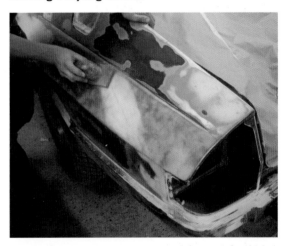

Sanding over guide coat.

Use guide coat to help make any last-minute adjustments.

Use your sanding block at 45 degrees to the panel.

Make sure you check your sandpaper is not clogged.

Let the paper do the work here, so avoid too much pressure and rub in a long, fluid motion. When you are using a block, change direction frequently – do three or four strokes along the panel, then up the panel, then at 45 degrees, then at 45 degrees the other way. If you sand in the same direction, you will create sanding score marks that you will be able to see through your paint, though these should be noticeable with a guide coat.

If you are dealing with a particularly difficult low or high spot, you may rub through to the layer below (you will know because you will have used a different colour). Stop immediately. To avoid contamination with primer dust, do not reapply primer immediately. You may rub through the primer again, so fix all the small areas in one hit under paint booth conditions.

Remember to check your paper regularly too. It easily gets clogged (to rectify this tap it on a hard surface, but not your car) and will eventually wear and stop working.

Once the primer has been sanded using a 240-grit paper, go around the car again using the same sanding motion with a less coarse production paper like 320 grit, then repeat again with 500 grit before you apply paint.

SANDING CURVES

Once you have got the hang of sanding and the sort of pressure you need to apply, you can start preparing your curved surfaces. If you do not pay attention to styling lines the car can look fat and shapeless, so it is an essential part of the process.

Tackling the curved areas allows you to be creative with the sanding blocks you use. You can make a sanding block out of anything hard and dry that matches the curve or crease you want to prepare – from broom handle to a rolling pin. Wrap some paper round it, and begin sanding. Don't make your strokes too short on these tricky sections, or you may dig a hole in the primer.

CUT THE EDGES (AND SOME CORNERS)

Edges can pose a big problem because it is incredibly easy to cut too much primer back. Use a forgiving 320-grit production paper very gently to remove any imperfections, then finish with a 500 grit. Also, there is no point sanding around edges or curves where trim pieces, rubbers, handles or light fixtures will be bolted on, so gently remove the guide coat with a light paper like 500 grit.

Sanding curves requires care.

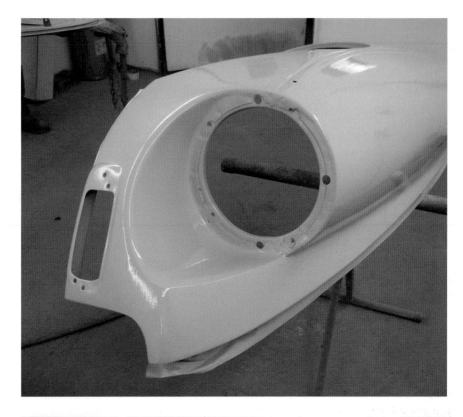

Always sand near, but not up to, an edge.

WHAT TO DO WITH LOW SPOTS

Once you have sanded your car using a guide coat, you will notice areas where the paint remains. It could be a sanding scratch or a small ding that you missed during the initial prep stage. Some primers allow stoppers to be applied over the top of them, so using the methods outlined in Chapter 4, mix some up, apply it to the area, re-prime it and re-sand. Make sure you re-check that the panel is fit for painting by using a guide coat when you sand.

ADDITIONAL WAYS TO STOP RUST APPEARING AT THE PRIMER STAGE

Using a selection of supporting products, there are ways to further prevent rust creeping in at the primer stage. You should try and incorporate as many of these as possible, especially in European climates. Even if you are only using your car on high days and holidays, you are bound to encounter rain or puddles, which will eventually damage a car if it is left unprotected.

SEAM SEALER

Most rust problems begin at the seams – this is the easiest path for water to take, and seam sealer failure can lead to water and other contaminants getting trapped between spot-welded panels (panels held together by spots of weld, rather than a seam of weld).

If you stripped your car back to bare metal, you will have encountered it already, but if your vehicle is more than twenty years old, you should replace any seam sealer as a matter of course as this deteriorates with age.

The easiest material to use is polyurethane (PU) sealant, which is available from your local paint supplier and comes in tubes designed to be used with a special sealant gun (or caulking gun, which is just like a wood glue gun). You will not be able to sand it so be careful when you lay it down; but you can paint over it.

You can apply a bead of sealant over self-etching primer, and while you may be tempted to only seal

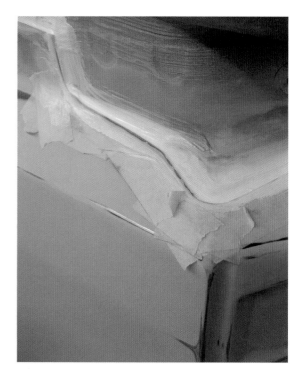

Seam sealer should be replaced as a matter of course.

Use a caulking gun to apply it.

Applying a bead of
seam sealer over
primer.

Additional seam
sealer can be
applied between the
wings and bodywork.

the panels originally seam sealed at the factory, you should make every effort to seal every seam you can find. But be sure to make a neat job of this, as any small gaps in the sealant can let water in behind the joint that will eventually fester and turn into rust. To get a nice, neat finish, put on your latex gloves and dip your index finger into some paint thinners, then run it across the sealant after you have applied it, as if you are grouting by hand. Use cellulose thinner if your primer is synthetic based, and synthetic thinners if your primer is cellulose based – this will prevent any nasty chemical reactions.

If you are painting an older car, the chances are it will have separate wings – when it comes to reassembly after you have put the primer on the panel, use seam sealant to close the gap between inner and outer panels as best you can by applying it to any gaps from both sides. This is something that did not always happen at the factory, but it will help you mitigate the chances of rust appearing because any overlapping panels are water traps.

ANTI-STONECHIP PRIMER

First and foremost, you should check with your supplier that an anti-stonechip primer is compatible with your paint and primer system. If you can use it, it provides a very durable plasticized coating that remains flexible after it has hardened, so stones tend to bounce off the surface as opposed to chipping the paint off. It also has excellent sound-deadening properties. As opposed to some under-body anti-gravel coatings, it is designed to be painted over with top-coat; it leaves a heavily orange-peeled finish so is only suitable for application under wheel arches or on sill and lower valance sections. Very little light will reach these areas, so it should remain hidden from sight unless it is closely inspected.

You can buy it in an aerosol but, because it is a thick coating, an aerosol nozzle will get clogged very quickly. For the best results buy a kit with its own air-line feed or one with a pneumatic gun attachment. These cost between £10 and £70 and are reusable

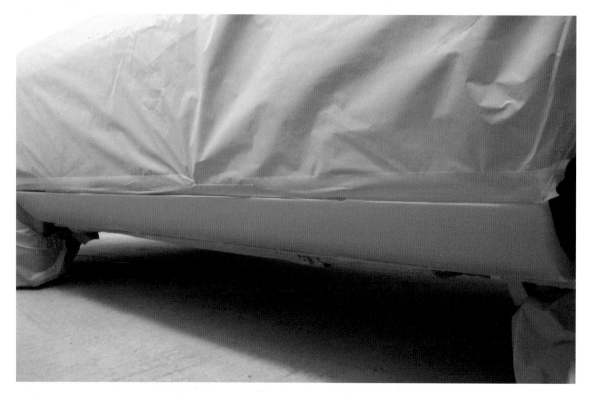

Anti-stonechip primer is not pretty so restrict usage to the underside.

Avoid stonechip primer in an aerosol without an air line feed or pneumatic attachment.

after cleaning. If you buy it as a two-part gun/primer kit, it is a good idea to heat the primer in a bucket of warm water to slightly thin it for easier mixing and application.

Make sure you shake the can after it has been warmed as anti-stonechip primers tend to settle into a thick gloop at the bottom, then just apply the gun and begin spraying. Start with hidden areas like the inner wheel arches to get used to using the heavier material.

If you are using an air-fed gun, spray at around 80psi (though pressures will be listed on the tin itself, so check these first). If you try and use the paint at too high a pressure, the tin can explode or start bubbling from the tin's seams, so be extremely careful.

In terms of coverage, you should get around 1m2 from each 1.0ltr tin – to coat the inside of four wings, the lower sill sections and a boot floor, expect to use between four and five tins.

OTHER PRIMERS

This is an at-a-glance glossary of primer products you may encounter – some should be avoided:

Red Oxide Also known as red lead, it should be avoided as the active ingredient is lead tetroxide and, as with all lead paints, can cause lead poisoning. However, most new primers marketed as red oxide do not contain lead and the colour is just a pigment added. Be sure to check with your supplier. If the source is unknown, dispose of it in accordance to your local guidelines.

Zinc Phosphate Most adhesive primers tend to contain some zinc, but the zinc component does not offer any galvanizing protection. The job of the zinc is to bond with the metal.

Galvanizing Primers Primers that contain around 90 per cent zinc offer galvanizing protection. However, their adhesive properties are poor, so you

Red oxide primer.

Zinc phosphate primer.

Use cellulose thinners to test a primer's quality.

will need to apply it directly onto very rough bare metal that has been sand or shot blasted.

Rust Neutralizing Primers These tend to contain phosphoric acid that reacts with exposed rust to create black iron phosphate – this neutralizes the uppermost layer of rust. If you have prepared your panels properly, you will not need this – all rust should be removed until you reach shiny metal, at which point you can use a more effective primer like acid etch.

Primer on Replacement Panels If you have had to buy new body panels from an original equipment manufacturer – or from the manufacturer itself – they will generally be coated in decent etching primer that will not need to be removed before

painting. However, if they are pattern parts, they may not be as durable. The best way to test them is with cellulose thinners. If you can remove the coating, it is not suitable. You can also gently rub an inconspicuous area with a coin – if it comes off, you will need to strip it back and apply a high quality primer.

Rust Sealers They do not kill rust, but provide a hardy barrier to keep moisture and air away, which prevents further corrosion. Products like the popular POR-15 polyurethane sealer can be brushed directly onto metalwork and cure with exposure to moisture. These are designed for under-body use, and should not be used on surface panels.

Now you can start the fun bit – painting your car.

CHAPTER EIGHT

PAINTING

This chapter answers the following questions:

• How should I work around my work space?
• How do I spray my car and panels with colour?
• What do I do immediately after my car is painted?

This is it – the first time you get to see your car in its brand-new coat of paint. The job might seem intimidating, but with a little practice and familiarity with the tools you are using, you will be able to transform your vehicle.

TOOLS AND MATERIALS FOR THIS CHAPTER

Panel Stands Dedicated products are best for this, but they are expensive, and if you only plan to use them once it is difficult to justify the expense. Also, there is no reason not to use other stable, flat objects to balance panels on, like oil drums, old chairs, and pallets.

Lint-Free Cloths This is to tie on top of your paint cup to stop any drips. These are available from any good paint supplier, and are absorbent. They look thicker than a normal cloth and have a spongy texture.

Panel Wipes These are lint-free wipes that are available from many different manufacturers. You can find them on the shelf at all good paint suppliers and should always keep a stock of them. You will need to dab them with degreaser or pre-paint degreaser, also known as panel wipe.

Tack Cloth This cloth is the last thing you will wipe your panel with before you paint it. It is a sticky cloth that picks up any remaining dust motes or particles of dirt. Each one will be individually sealed and should be sufficient for wiping down the panels on a whole car. They can also be used between coats of paint (once the paint has dried) to remove any particles that have settled on the panel.

Panel Wipe This liquid removes all dirt and sticky residue from the surface before you wipe the panel with a tack cloth. It is a solvent, so evaporates quickly, but this also means that you should check it is compatible with your paint system.

Your Full Paint System Prepare all the ingredients of your paint system as if you are cooking a meal. All of the products should be clearly labelled, so make sure they are facing outwards so you can see what you are picking up. Your products should all have lids too, so there is no need not to remove them from storage.

Paint Safety Kit You will need to put on your steel toe-cap boots, protective coverall, latex gloves, respiration equipment and protective glasses if you are not using a full-face respirator. If you need to re-familiarize yourself with the products, turn to Chapter 2.

NOW YOU CAN BEGIN PAINTING

This is the fun part – you can finally turn that primed bodyshell into something that resembles a finished, painted car that will last for decades to come.

Although you will have practised spraying with your primer gun or tip, and learned how to achieve the best possible spray pattern, you should re-familiarize yourself because proper application is just as

Painting scrap parts for practice.

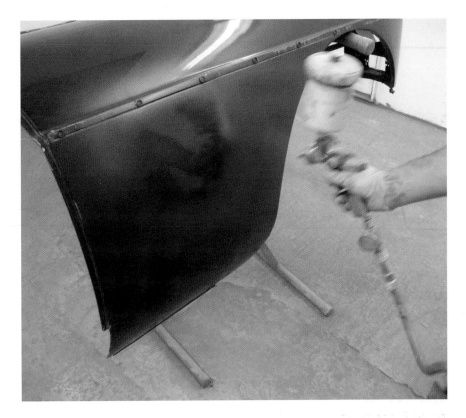

important as proper preparation and using the best materials. If you can, practise with some scrap parts (you can prime them with an aerosol) and any cheap paint you can get your hands on.

Learn how too much paint causes runs and sags, and spray the panel horizontally and vertically so you know how the material behaves in these situations. Basically, practise every circumstance that you anticipate you will come across when you paint your car, and try and make as many mistakes here as you can, so you can avoid them on your perfectly prepared shell.

You can also practise wet and dry sanding (we will come to those subjects shortly), and repairing scratches. Use your finger to test if the paint is dry so you know how long to wait, then try and repair any fingerprints you have left. You probably will not have to do this, but also have a go at removing all the paint using the stripping techniques specified in Chapter 3 just in case the worst happens.

This is also a good opportunity to check that your ventilation system, compressed air supply, gun cleaning and safety gear are up to scratch. If you notice that

anything is untoward, repair or replace the necessary parts. This is also a good time to revisit the paint mixing guideline set out in Chapter 5. Remember to mix everything on your workbench and strain it as you pour it into the gun. Once you can paint a scrap panel perfectly, you should start getting to work on your vehicle.

Also consider timings. To get the best out of all paint systems, you should follow the time guidelines specified by the manufacturer. All will be fairly tight, and incorporate curing times, which will require you to commit at least a few solid days to the job. Make sure you are able to do this as leaving it for too long between coats can cause problems. You should also make a checklist with rough timings that allows you cross off jobs once they have been completed. Make it as big as you can and stick it on the wall near a clock, this way you will so you can always stay focused on the job regardless of any distractions, and stick as closely as you can to your timings. Also, some hardeners in paints can go off in as little as ten minutes, so you must be ready to paint immediately after you have mixed your system.

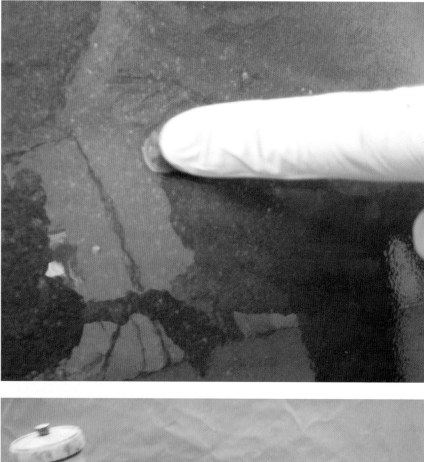

Pressing a finger into soft paint to gauge if it is dry.

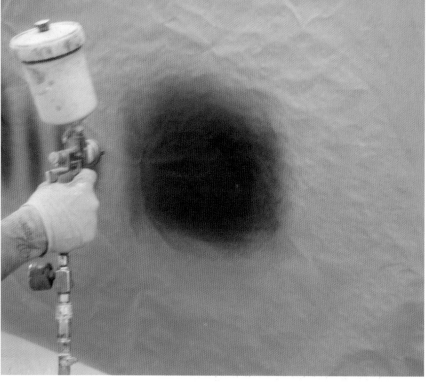

Use a piece of paper to test your spray pattern.

Before you begin mixing and straining your paint, you should stick a test panel near the area where you intend to paint. This does not have to be an actual body panel, rather a sheet of wide masking paper, or clean cardboard that allows you to quickly spray onto the wall to check your spray pattern and volume settings are correct, and to make any necessary adjustments before painting the car. If adjustments on the gun fail to fix the problem, you can briefly disconnect the gun from the air supply hose and clean it.

WORKING AROUND YOUR SPACE

As mentioned in Chapter 2, you will need at least 3m (10ft) around whatever part you are painting (including the full shell) to get the best possible results. The reason for this being that your gun should always be perpendicular to the surface being painted, at between 15 and 20cm (6 and 10in) away from it, oth-

erwise you risk putting on too much paint (which causes runs) or too little (which causes dry spots – areas that are not properly covered by the material).

Think about how your paint will apply – if your workshop's limitations mean that it is not comfortable to avoid swinging the gun in an arc – where the paint will be too thick in the middle of the arc and too thin at each end of it, you need to reconsider where to do the job. As well as issues with application, if an outer layer of paint dries more quickly than inner layers, the solvent evaporating from the inside can cause problems for your finish. Also, if the gun is tilted towards the surface, the fan pattern will not be uniform. Chances are, you will have to kneel down at some point to achieve this, and you must have the space to do so. You will need plenty of room to inspect the panel you have painted during the process.

Make sure you are happy with the space you have before you paint.

It is essential to have room to kneel down.

PANEL STANDS

If you have properly prepared your car, the doors, wings, bonnet and boot will be removed. To paint them, you will need to put them on a stand of some sort that gives you access to the whole surface, that will support its weight and will be completely stable. Professional body shops use specialist panel stands and holding racks, but they can be expensive so you can be creative with what you use. If you wish to paint smaller parts, unwound coat hangers can be used to hang them, and old tables are ideal for holding parts with large flat plains like bonnets and doors (just as long as all the surfaces you want to paint are exposed).

PAINTING FLEXIBLE PARTS

Since the seventies, car manufacturers have used a lot more plastic parts to drive down manufacturing costs and reduce weight. While the DIY-er can

As with paper stands, you do not need to restrict panel stands to costly professional products.

not be able to paint over some plastics at all – a handful of materials are unable to be repainted once the original primer seal has been broken because they too sensitive to solvents. You will need to replace them with new parts.

The best way to check what you need is to research the type of plastic you have on your car by consulting your local dealership or an owners' club. If they don't have the information, and your vehicle manufacturer is still in business, most major car makers have a dedicated heritage department, and will be able to deal with these enquiries. These tend to be based in the marque's original home country, but all should have an English-speaking agent. Search online for contact details. Once you have the necessary information, ask your paint supplier what they recommend.

PUT ON YOUR SAFETY GEAR

To prevent any dirt or dust from everyday clothing landing on the panel, you should change into your full painting kit before you go into your workspace Now give yourself a brush down and go into the booth.

You may need a paint additive for flexible components.

achieve a smooth, glossy finish that equals painted metal on these materials, the process involved to get the best results is slightly different and requires some thought before you start laying down your material.

Plastics used for automotive applications range from acrylonitrile butadiene styrene (ABS), polypropylene, reaction injection moulded plastic (RIM) and sheet moulded compounds (SMC), and are used for everything from bumpers to trim pieces. Unlike steel, they are quite flexible, and you may need specialist additives that allow some flex in the paint before you apply it.

Most base coat/clear coat urethane systems should be able to move a little, but other materials will require additional ingredients to avoid problems once cured and mounted on the car. Also, adhesion can be an issue with some plastic, which will require a dedicated product. While it is a rare issue, you may

Remember to put your painting gear on in the right order.

FINAL PANEL PREPARATIONS

You should have a fully primed panel that has been completely repaired, but it can pick up grease and dirt after just a few minutes of storage. It can also pick up dirt and dust from you and your clothes, even if you have brushed yourself down thoroughly. Give it one last clean with a panel wipe – this will remove the wax and grease. Wipe it once with panel wipe that has some degreasing solvent on it (this, confusingly, is called panel wipe as well), then wipe it again with a dry panel wipe.

Once you have degreased and cleaned, use a fresh tack cloth on the surface. This will pick up the last remaining surface contaminants, so you should only do this just before you paint because due to ambient motes you simply cannot keep the surface spotless for long.

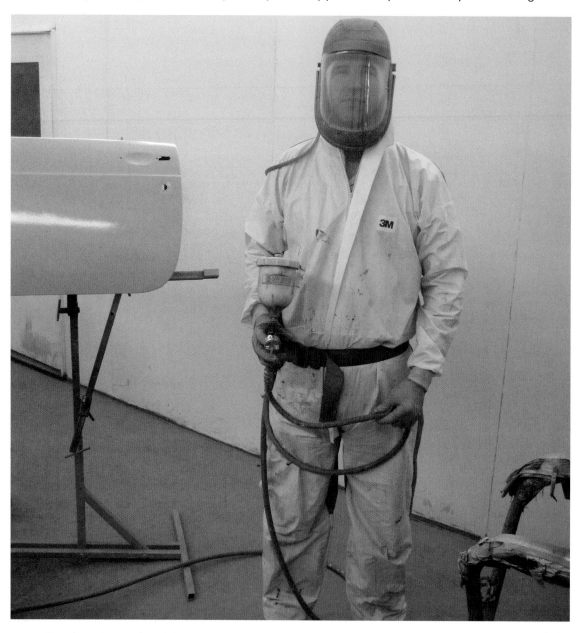

You will need to continue preparing your panels right up to the moment you paint.

MAKE A PLAN OF ATTACK

Plan to lay a border of paint around your panel, then fill in the middle. This way, any overspray you generate that lands in the centre section can form part of the final surface, meaning you have to use less material before the paint droplets spring into a sheet. If you try and paint the centre section first then hit the edges, overspray can land on your carefully painted middle section and cause a rough surface. You should only start filling in the area once you are happy with the coverage and thickness of the border.

If you are painting a panel like a wing, the chances are it will not have a uniform flatness, and may include flared areas. You should still follow the border-then-fill mantra, but make sure you are ready to change the angle of your gun so the tip always remains perpendicular to the area you wish to paint.

CURING TIME

You have to wait for each layer of paint to cure and the solvents to evaporate before applying the next layer. This is called the flash time. If you are impatient, the evaporating solvents from the lower layers pass through the upper layers, which can cause anything from cracking, blistering, sagging and lifting on the top coat.

Every paint system available with have a clearly marked flash time on the information sheet that comes with it, and they will differ between suppliers and coatings. A clear coat, for example, may have a greater flash time than an undercoat, and vice versa. Do not leave it till you have painted your first coat to find out how long it is – that way you can plan your timings.

AVOID DRIPPING

The last thing you want is any paint material dripping from your cup onto the panel when you are spraying. To avoid the possibility of this happening, tie a lint-free cloth onto the top of your paint cup. Even if the instructions that come with your gun claims that it is drip-free, you should take this precaution as a cheap and easy insurance policy.

Make sure you inspect all areas of the gun before spraying.

NOW BEGIN PAINTING

Now you are absolutely sure you have the space and equipment for the job, have mixed the perfect paint, turned on your lighting and, if applicable, heating systems, you can begin spraying. Remember that the long and short of the painting process is that you are trying to make lots of the tiny droplets that land on the surface of your panel spring into a singular sheet of paint that covers the area in an even thickness. Too much paint causes runs and sags; too little and you won't get the uniform sheet of paint.

Start with an easy, flat panel like a door or bonnet. With it placed on your stand, lay down a tack coat, which is effectively a thin dusting of paint. It will begin to dry and become sticky, so when you put your thicker, second coat onto the tacky layer it will adhere better. Never try and put a full coat of paint onto a primed panel because there is good chance it will run or sag.

When you apply the paint, remember to hold the gun horizontally to the surface, and squeeze the trigger

Make sure your body is in the right position to maximize your paint finish quality.

with the gun a few inches from the edge of the panel – if you start your pass on the edge of the panel you will cause paint build-up on the edges. Make sure your gun is also positioned so the spray fan overlaps either the edge of the panel or the masked edge by around 50 per cent, so half of the material isn't being applied to the panel, or is being applied onto the masking paper.

Your arm should be bent at an angle of 45 degrees at the elbow. Now move the gun along at around 30cm/sec (12in/sec), ensuring that your gun remains the same distance from the surface at all times by locking your wrist in place and walking alongside the panel. Do not use your arm to reach the extremes of your panel as this will affect the angle of your spray pattern.

Once you have made one pass, make sure the next pass overlaps it by around 50 per cent, and be careful to ensure your gun is the same distance from the panel – remember, between 15 and 20cm (6 and 10in) is ideal. Also, be careful not to try and do too

much with each pass. The trap novice painters often fall into is applying too much material because it looks glossy and very close to a finished, polished car – but after a few minutes, imperfections like runs and sags form. These are not an unmitigated disaster, but you will need to spend a great deal of time correcting them (doing so is covered later in this chapter).

SPRAYING CLEAR COAT

If you want to apply a metallic finish, or your paint system includes a clear coat from the off, the chances are your system will include a clear coat. In some cases it can reduce the amount of colour you use, and in others it simply provides a more hard-wearing surface for more delicate finishes. It is also a good way to disguise harsh paint lines from racing stripes or other custom touches by adding a smoother layer on the surface, and in the same way it can be used to blend old paint in with new.

Remember though, considering the amount of sanding, preparation, and potential for solvent incompatibility and the subsequent reactions, you should never just add a new layer of clear coat to a pre-existing and damaged clear coat.

The application process itself is exactly the same as painting on colour – you need to keep your gun between 15 and 20cm (6 and 10in) from the panel, overlap each pass by around 50 per cent and spray at around 30cm/sec (12in/sec). The key consideration here is the flash time. Just like every other layer, you will need to make sure the solvents are completely evaporated before you add a fresh coat, or you may find you have nasty surface imperfections to deal with, and sorting them out properly can involve stripping the clear coat back to the colour substrate. You can afford to be slightly less stringent with overspray though, because clear dries to a see-through finish. That said, you should have got yourself into the habit of avoiding it where possible when spraying on your colour, so chances are it will not be an issue.

WATCHING PAINT DRY

This is a tedious component to the painting process, but it is absolutely essential that your car is in the right place for the right amount of time after you

It may be boring, but adhering to the correct flash times is absolutely essential.

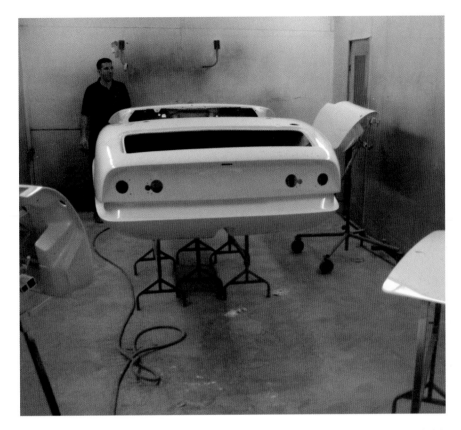

have laid down your paint. Much as you did when you painted the car, you need to ensure that the work area is free from any dust or dirt – if not, debris can contaminate the wet paint, and in extreme examples this will mean you have to strip it back and start again. You will also need to ensure that the temperature is carefully monitored. Guidelines for the ideal conditions your paint should dry in will be found in the information that comes with your paint system.

There are usually two options: air drying and forced drying. The latter applies to commercial paint shops that need to remove a car from their booth (this is where the pros dry their cars) as quickly as possible so they can get the next car in. If you have rented a booth from a paint shop, then this information will be useful. However, if you have converted your own workspace into an area suitable for painting, you can follow an air guide flash time.

If you have invested in heat lamps, be sure not to turn them on while the paint is still wet. Pretty much all systems will require a short amount of time to

air dry under ordinary conditions so all the solvents can evaporate from the paint. If you rush the process with heat, they may evaporate too quickly, which can stain the top coat.

However, there is just as much potential for doing your paint job damage by leaving it to dry for too long. Many systems have a brief window in which you are expected to add another coat or wet sand the paint. If you take too long, you may have to carefully key the surface with an abrasive to apply another layer, which carries risks of damaging the final finish with sanding marks.

At this stage, keep all of your masking tape, fine line tape and paper in situ, because you will need it in place during the following stages. If you remove it too quickly, you may also take some of the material off with the masking tape – this is called stringing and can be extremely damaging.

With your basic paint job applied, you can begin to add stripes and other custom touches, or if things have not gone your way, skip to Chapter 10 for some disaster relief.

CHAPTER NINE

STRIPES AND OTHER CUSTOM TOUCHES

This chapter answers the following questions:

• How do I apply stripes and/or two-tone finishes to my vehicle?
• What paint should I use to coachline my vehicle?
• Can I add these effects after I have finished painting?
• How do I add a coachline to my car?

If you have finished painting but want to add some additional features or recreate some original coachlines or graphics, this chapter will guide you through the best ways to do so.

PLANNING YOUR ADDITIONAL PAINT FEATURES

Whether it is a simple coachline or full-blown two-tone paint job, you should include this in your paint job itinerary from the outset. However, if you finish painting your vehicle and decide that you would like to add an extra dimension to the finish, it is entirely possible to do so, though you will need to sand and re-prime the area before you add colour. This may give you some problem because there will be a noticeable thickness difference between the two layers. It is far better to two-tone a vehicle from the same stripped, prepared surface and primed substrate.

As with all aspects of painting, adding another layer of colour to your vehicle will mean re-masking, re-preparing the surface, ensuring your work space is clean and temperature-controlled, and checking that any

Additional features add personality to your car.

If you are planning a two-tone paint finish, you must use the car's proportions wisely to find your split line.

materials you use are compatible; otherwise you risk compromising the finish you have applied underneath.

You will also need to make sure that the underlying paint has been given its correct flash time, and is completely dry. Otherwise you will have to deal with everything from major defects, to over-soft paint peeling off when masking tape is removed.

A final consideration is the type of paint system you use. Some are better suited to this job, especially those that include a base coat and separate clear lacquer. By using a system like this, you can apply a number of coats of lacquer, and then if any over-spray of the second colour hits your first colour, you use wet and dry paper to remove it without rubbing through to the colour layer. You will also be able to disguise the split line well by adding multiple coats of lacquer over the finished two-tone vehicle and buffing to a high shine.

TWO-TONE PAINT

Several cars are finished with differing upper and lower paint colours at the factory. However, you will need to study the vehicle before you begin painting so you can see exactly how the two colours are divided.

Generally, manufacturers will use trims or styling creases to separate the colours, and in addition some older vehicles may use coachlines too (we will come to those shortly). It is crucial to see where these separations lie before you begin removing the old paint. Take plenty of pictures and make notes or drawings so it is as close to the original as possible. Pay particular attention to areas where the primary colour overlaps with the secondary colour, and which structural areas of the body, like door jambs and the engine bay, are finished in what. It seems like a minor consideration, but you would be surprised how awkward and homespun your car can look if these subtle details differ from the original paint job.

HOW TO ACHIEVE
A TWO-TONE FINISH

If you decide that you want to undertake a two-tone paint job on a car that was never originally given one, you should study a factory two-tone for guidance. There are some basic rules:

Follow the Original Body Lines Use a styling crease or curve in the bodywork to separate the two colours. But be careful which line you chose.

Colour Belt Positioning If you plan on painting a darker colour below a lighter colour, beware that positioning the break too high will make your car look shorter and fatter and the roof line lower. Conversely, positioning it too low will make the vehicle look longer. This can be an issue even if you follow the vehicle's bodylines. It is very easy for there to be an imbalance in the look of your car.

Deviate at Your Peril Some custom two-tone finishes, like a diagonal slash, may give the car a sense of speed and motion, but remember that they are very subjective and may affect your vehicle's resale or insurance value.

Rule of Thirds The most successful custom two-tone paint jobs on traditional three-box vehicles (named because the design looks roughly like a box for the bonnet, a box for the cabin and a box for the boot) tend to break the paint roughly a third of the way down the shoulder line. This should balance the two colours. Usually a piece of trim will be fitted along a car's flanks that will make identifying this break obvious.

Where to Split the Paint If you are using a trim piece to cover the split, make sure you divide the differing colours evenly along the line that separates them. If you have, say, an inch-thick section of trim, you should mask your car so half an inch is in the upper colour and half an inch is in the lower colour. Most vehicles will have holes punched in to the panel for the trim fixtures – use them to draw a line between the two colours. Before you begin masking, double-check your line by loosely mounting the trim to ensure the split line will be concealed. Be extremely careful if the trim is narrower as this greatly reduces your margin for error.

What to Paint First To avoid giving yourself too much work, paint the area that is easiest to mask first. That way you can lay down your colour, leave it for the correct flash and drying time, then quickly mask up the rest of the car and begin applying the next colour.

COACHLINES AND PINSTRIPING

This has several meanings in the world of car painting – it can be a simple, single line that runs along the body of a car or it can be a custom design using roughly $1/8$in lines of paint or vinyl.

You can buy pinstriping vinyl stickers, or you can have a go at pinstriping your car the traditional way – an art now reserved for classic vehicles and luxury cars like Rolls-Royces and Bentleys. But the finish will be far superior to any sticker-based product, and far more hard wearing. That said, pinstriping requires a little bit of planning. If you are applying accent pinstriping along a bodyline, make sure you paint to one side of the raised body line to avoid it rubbing off.

Making a good job of this requires a special brush, special paint and a tremendous amount of patience and skill, so make sure you have had extensive practice before you attempt anything on your freshly painted car.

The most common paint for this application is called One-Shot and it is relatively inexpensive. Also, you will not need a great deal to do, say, one or two coachlines around your vehicle, so the half-litre tins it comes in will be more than enough for a car. They are also available in several colours premixed. If you want your own colour, buy red, yellow and blue, and you should be able to come up with your own unique tint easily. Be warned about the latter though – if it rubs off, it may be difficult to duplicate.

Enamel paint like One-Shot is compatible with pretty much all paint surfaces, though just to be absolutely sure you should ask your paint supplier. Make sure you also have odourless mineral spirits to clean up any errant paint.

PINSTRIPING BRUSH

You will find it extremely difficult to lay down a decent pin stripe if you are using anything other than a dedicated pinstriping product, like a Mack Series 10 Squirrel Hair Sword Striping Brush. When you purchase the brush, it will not be ready to use immediately. First you dip it in a very small pot of engine oil then rinse it in mineral spirits. This helps it to keep

Coachlines are common on everything from Rovers to Rolls-Royces.

its shape. With the bristles of the brush flattened on a flat surface, use a new razor blade to trim the tips of the longest bristles at 90 degrees to the brush. You should only remove 2mm at most. Holding the brush correctly is extremely important too – you should grip it with your thumb and index finger just above the wrapping (called the ferrule). The bristles will have a flat and curved side like a sword – the curved side should be facing your arm.

PALETTE YOUR PAINT

As with ordinary paints, you will need to thin your pinstriping materials, but you should do this on a palette. You do not need a specialist product for this

– an old magazine or plastic lid should be sufficient. Add a two-pence piece-sized dollop of paint onto your pallet and a drop of your reducer. Load the bristles up with material by wiping it in the paint thoroughly, then re-shape the bristles so they look like a sword again.

PULL A LINE

Hold the brush with the curved side of the bristles facing your arm and stick out your little finger for balance. Lock your hand, wrist and arm, allow the brush to bend slightly as you place it on the surface, then pull it brush towards you while keeping the bristles at a constant position to the surface, otherwise the line will get thicker or thinner. Practise on a piece of paper, running lines parallel to each other. If you are concerned that you will find it difficult to achieve an arrow-straight line, you can buy specialist pinstriping masking tape – effectively two pieces of plastic Fine Line-like tape on the same reel of tape – for you to paint between. It is extremely flexible, so you can follow tricky curves if needs be.

THE PINSTRIPING TOOL

Products are available from manufacturers like Beugler that remove the need for a brush. That said, mastering them requires a fair bit of practice. You pour the same one-shot enamel into a small cylinder, under which there is a head with a wheel. When you rotate the wheel, paint is taken from the cylinder and is laid onto the surface in an even line via the wheel. They also have balancing arms, which you can use to slide next to a panel so the brush remains perpendicular to the panel. This is metal, so you should only use this on masked paintwork, or use magnetic guide stripes that are also available from Beugler.

STICKERS AND VINYL

Some vehicles will have had a sticker or graphic applied at the factory. If you want to recreate this you should make sure the panel is completely cured, then clean the area with fast-drying wax and grease remover. Avoid using household spray cleaners because they can leave behind a residue or oily substance that affects how the graphic adheres.

Decide how you want to centre your sticker. If it is writing, make sure you measure the first and last letters (not the sticker backing, as they are not always cut straight) from the top or bottom so they are the same distance from a panel crease. Always rely on a bodyline for this, not a spirit-level – because most cars have slightly raked suspension, the sticker may appear crooked if it is perfectly level.

Take a misting spray bottle, put no more than one small drop of soap in it, fill it with water, then shake. Very, very lightly spray the area you want to apply the sticker. Most factory decals will be supplied sandwiched between two sheets – a clear sheet and a smooth paper

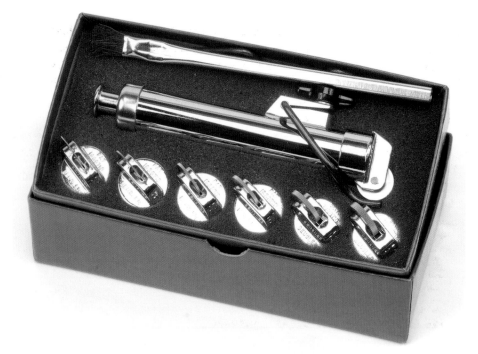

A Beugler pinstriping tool.

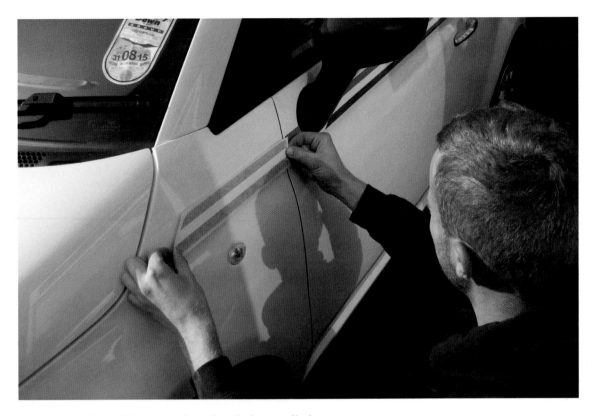

Stickers need careful positioning when being applied.

sheet. Remove around three inches of the paper sheet, exposing the sticky side of the graphic. Now slowly apply the graphic, pressing it on to the panel while peeling away the backing paper. With the graphic applied and while holding on to the clear sheet, use a credit card held at 45 degrees to scrape out any air bubbles. The mist of soapy water will allow you to do this without damaging the vinyl, but the sticker may slightly shift if you press too hard, so be careful.

If you can, leave your vehicle in bright sunshine to help the drying process. If this is not possible, avoid using a heat gun to speed up the drying process or it may melt the vinyl. You should wait at least an hour before you try and remove the clear tape.

With everything applied and all your custom touches made, you are ready to start turning your panels back into a car again.

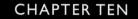
DISASTER RELIEF FOR THE AMATEUR PAINTER

This chapter answers the following questions:

• My paint has a defect. What is it?
• What caused it?
• How do I fix it?

A run or sag.

When you come to paint your car, there is a chance that you will face a few difficulties. Whether it is a small run or full-blown peeling, there are actions you can take to correct it, or at least minimize the damage. Stay calm and keep painting.

RUNS OR SAGS

These look like a drip of paint running down your panel, or U-shaped sag, and form most easily on vertical panels because gravity pulls down even slightly too much material.

CAUSE

You are either applying too much paint or the material itself is not working properly. The former can be caused by insufficient air pressure, not leaving enough distance between the gun and surface, or excessive overlap between each pass. The latter may be a result of the paint and hardener ratio, the temperature of your unit and material, or because you have not left enough time between coats for the paint to cure.

HOW TO FIX IT

Some small runs and sags can be flattened with wet and dry paper after the paint has cured.

Alternatively, isolate the damaged panel, remove the paint, and respray.

ORANGE PEEL

This, unsurprisingly, relates to your paint finish looking like orange peel. If you look at a normal production car up close, it will have a little orange peel texture to the paint, but too much can ruin reflections in your panel.

CAUSE

You may be applying too much paint, which means you should check your air pressure and ensure the distance between the gun and panel is not too close. It may also be the temperature – remember, more heat does not mean a better paint job. If it dries too fast, this is one of the symptoms. Alternatively, it could be the paint itself – if the material does not have enough reducing solvent, it will apply to the panel like this.

HOW TO FIX IT

Depending on the paint you use, and the extent of the orange peel texture, you can buff this out with either fine wet and dry paper, or by using a mild cutting compound and dual-action polisher.

DRY SPRAY

Instead of a smooth, glossy finish, your paint may cure to a dull, rough texture.

CAUSE

Depending on how rough and how dry the cured paint feels, this could be something as simple as overspray or it could mean you are not applying enough material. In any case, check the material is flowing through the gun properly with your test paper, and that the air feed is not blocked. It may even be something as simple as holding the gun too far away from the panel.

HOW TO FIX IT

Sand down the affected area then respray, and remember to leave the recommended flash time, even if the finish is less than perfect. Use relatively aggressive wet and dry paper, like 800 grit, to give the panel plenty of bite for the paint you will apply on top.

FISH EYES

These are small, round indentations that look like little craters or fish's eyes.

CAUSE

These are the end result of a chemical reaction – this is the paint's response to anything from oil, grease, water or silicon wax to sanding dust. This reaction is indicative of a poorly cleaned panel or contaminated

Orange peel.

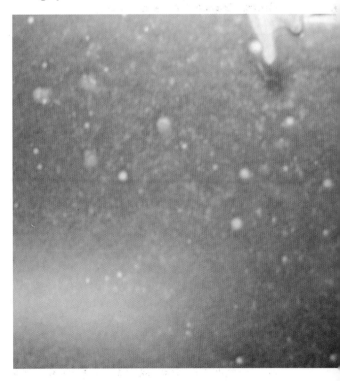

Fish eyes.

air supply, though it could be something as minor as eating greasy food or sweating in your spray area.

HOW TO FIX IT

After draining your air pressure regulator and cleaning your gun, apply light coats of basecoat until you have covered the imperfection. If this fails to work, you can mix in a special fish eye eliminator to your paint, though you must check that it is compatible with the system you are using.

DIRT INCLUSION

You will notice if any small specs of dirt have found their way onto your freshly painted panel by running your hand across the cured paint. If you feel any sharp bumps, you will need to remove them.

CAUSE

Typically, dirt particles will find their way to your panel because your spray area is not clean enough. There are several reasons for this. It could be poor air fil-

Dirt in dried paint.

tration, an inadequately prepared surface, unstrained paint or even dusty clothes. It may also be a static charge on the car's surface, which attracts dust.

HOW TO FIX IT

Your paint area should be completely dust-free, which may mean you need to slightly wet the walls and floors (though too much will add too much moisture, which can damage the finish). That includes you, too – make sure you wear a proper paint suit, as detailed in Chapter 1. If you think the problem is static-based, spray a little paint onto a practice panel then shine a torch to see if you can see if any dust gets drawn to the surface. If so, either attach the vehicle to an electrical earth or use some anti-static fluid. A little dirt is not usually a massive issue to remedy, and can be sanded with 800-grit wet and dry, then polished after the paint has fully hardened.

HIDING

In some cases, you may find that the paint finish does not cover up filler, primer or sealer, leaving it visible after the paint has cured.

CAUSE

This is usually caused by mixing too much thinner into your paint, so the colour does not sufficiently cover your repairs. Another cause is that the primer you have used is too dark for the top coat – this is rare, but can happen if you use very dark primer in a localized area then spray a very light colour on top.

HOW TO FIX IT

After you have checked your paint/thinner ratio, allow the material to dry and cure, then reapply until you can no longer see the darker area.

LIFTING

This is a fairly major problem, but is unlikely to happen if you use whole paint system as opposed to potentially incompatible products. If your substrate is either inappropriate or not cured enough to accept the top coat, the paint will wrinkle or crack.

Paint failing to cover up filler, primer or sealer.

CAUSE

You might come across this if your combination of primer, paint and thinners is incompatible. Exceptions are applying paint without leaving the correct flash time for previous layers or applying too much paint, though runs and sags usually appear long before the surface cracks.

HOW TO FIX IT

If you are absolutely sure that your paint systems are compatible, sand off the affected areas and respray. In severe cases, you will have to remove all of the paint right down to the substrate before you refinish to avoid any future contamination.

MATTING

After your paint has dried and all the solvents have evaporated, the surface does not look glossy and it feels dry.

CAUSE

Much like dry spray, the root of these problems tends to lie in too little paint thickness or poor airflow. It

Paint lifting.

Matted paint.

could also be caused by the baking (curing) process being interrupted if you are using a professional booth or by spraying in too high a humidity.

HOW TO FIX IT

Usually, this will be a sand-and-polish remedy. If the finish is still dry, check your paint ratios, make sure your airflow is sufficient and check with your paint system manufacturer's guidelines to ensure you are painting within its humidity parameters.

MOTTLING

This tends to be exclusive to metallic finishes and leaves a striped or spotty finish.

CAUSE

A number of things create this. First, check your material – you may not have mixed the paint sufficiently or used the correct thinner. It can also be caused by the gun – you may be holding it too close to the panel, using the incorrect amount of air pressure to feed

it or having an uneven spray pattern. It is also indicative of painting in weather outside your paint system's operational parameters, especially humidity and lower temperatures. Finally, much like other problems, it can also be indicative of too short a flash time.

HOW TO FIX IT

Allow the colour coat to cure, then apply a drier double coat or two single coats. If your paint system uses a clear coat and the effect is only noticeable after you have applied it, thoroughly dry it then sand it off and start again.

PEELING

Paint will literally peel from the surface because there it is not adhering to the primer or previous paint job underneath.

CAUSE

If this happens when you whip off the masking tape, you have not let the paint dry sufficiently. Otherwise,

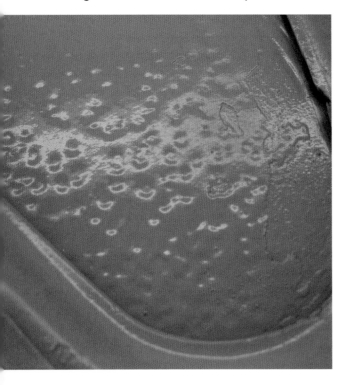

Mottled paint.

Peeling paint.

there are a number of causes. Presuming you are using a complete, compatible paint system, this is indicative of several problems: the metal may not have been properly sanded, you may not have used enough sealer, you have applied too much paint, the surface temperature was too high or low, your work area had too much condensation, the panel was not clean enough, you applied too much primer and failed to give it enough bite for the paint, or you did not leave enough flash time between coats.

HOW TO FIX IT

You will have to remove the peeling paint, and around three additional inches of paint from the area that surrounds it before refinishing.

POPPING

They tend to form in groups and look like lots of little pinholes in the paint.

CAUSE

This is usually the result of trapped solvents escaping through the upper layers of paint. If you have fanned the wet paint instead of letting it cure properly, a surface film will dry, but the paint underneath will remain wet, and the solvents that would ordinarily evaporate evenly need to find a way out of the paint, so pop through to the surface. It can also be caused by moisture left on primed surfaces, moisture or oil in your air line, or too thick a top coat.

HOW TO FIX IT

Sand until the area is completely smooth, then re-apply your paint and let it dry un-fanned.

POLISHING MARKS

Once you have wet sanded or polished your car, you may find sections that are lighter or darker than the paint underneath, or edges that you burned through to the substrate below.

CAUSE

This is usually caused by over-eager painters. If the top coat is still soft, sanding and polishing compounds may leave blemishes on the surface. It can also be the result of using wet and dry paper that is too coarse.

HOW TO FIX IT

If you have noticed this early on, leave your car alone until you are absolutely sure the paint is dry. Now make sure you are using the correct sandpaper and, just to be safe, use polish that has no ammonia in it, then have another go.

OVERSPRAY

Paint from your gun falls onto a nearby surface, causing dry spots on the surface.

CAUSE

This is common problem and happens regularly, even to the professionals. Misdirecting spray droplets from your gun causes it and, even with the best HVLP unit,

Paint overspray.

it is almost guaranteed to affect your paint job in some way. That said, it is usually an extremely easy fix.

HOW TO FIX IT

Provided there is only a little overspray, use a mild polishing compound on a dual-action buffer with a foam pad. If this fails to lift it, use increasingly aggressive cutting compounds and, as a last resort, wet sand the area. Now check that your air pressure is not too high to avoid it happening again.

If overspray has landed on chrome surfaces, you should be able to lift it with chrome polish, otherwise use 0000 steel wool with polish. To get it off glass, try using a dab of your reducing solvent on a cloth. Be careful though – some windscreens are made with acrylic ingredients that can be damaged with 0000 steel wool.

SLOW DRYING

You have waited for the paint manufacturer's recommended time and your paint still refuses to dry.

CAUSES

Generally, impatience. But other things like using the wrong activator, incorrect mixing ratio, applying too much paint or poor drying conditions can be at fault.

HOW TO FIX IT

If the paint is not vulnerably wet, put your car in a warmer, more ventilated area. Otherwise, do what you can to ensure your booth gets as much ventilation as possible, but make sure this does not expose the vehicle to contaminants like dust and water.

WATER SPOTS

Small dots appear on the dry, cured paint that are considerably duller than the paint that surrounds them.

CAUSES

This is an after-paint problem and is usually caused by washing down your car in bright sunlight, or leaving it in the rain before it has fully hardened. In rare cases, using unsuitable thinners might also cause it.

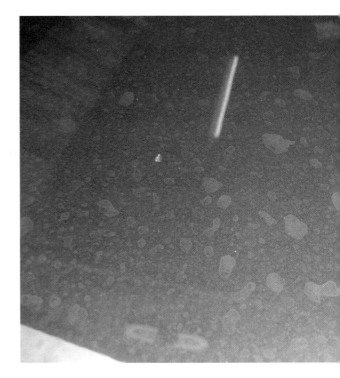

Water spots.

HOW TO FIX IT

Generally, you can fix water spots with some judicious polishing; though make sure you use a light compound. Also, make sure the paint is fully hardened and cured before you attack it, and keep it out of the rain.

CRACKING

It looks a lot like cracked mud in a dry pond and is often formed from lots of three-legged stars.

CAUSES

If you have applied too many top coats, or applied too thick a top coat, the excessive film thickness will be exposed to magnified stresses, which cause it to split. It could also be the result of poorly mixed paint, insufficient flash times or painting in temperatures that are either too hot or too cold. You may also have painted a flexible panel without using the correct additive that allows some flex.

Cracked paint.

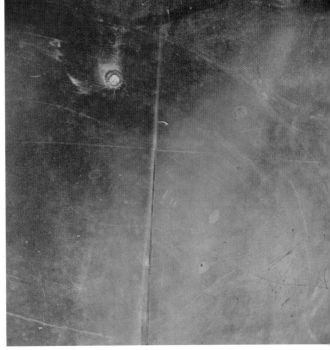

Yellowed paint.

HOW TO FIX IT

Unfortunately, you will have to remove all the affected areas and start again, in some cases sanding down to bare metal if the primer is also cracked.

YELLOWING

On systems that use a clear coat, you may find that it dries with a yellowy tint, making it look like you have mismatched the colour.

CAUSES

This could simply be mixing in the incorrect hardener, using different amounts of clear coat between the panels or contaminated materials. Usually, it is the latter. You can ruin clear coat just by leaving the lid off the can.

HOW TO FIX IT

You will need to let it dry, sand it off, and then start all over again.

CHAPTER ELEVEN

BEYOND THE PAINT BOOTH

This chapter answers the following questions:

• Should I wet sand my car?
• How do I machine-polish the paint?
• Which products are suitable at this stage?
• When I can I remove my masking paper?

Now you have rolled your painted car out of your spray booth, it is time to make some final adjustments to really make your top coat pop. Gentle sanding and polishing will give your finish the final boost it needs to look as good as new.

TOOLS AND MATERIALS FOR THIS CHAPTER

Wet and Dry If you are buying 25-sheet packs, you should aim to get one pack of 1,200 grit, one of 1,500 and one of 2,000. That will easily be enough to flat a car, probably two. Smaller paint suppliers will sell you sheets individually, if needs be.

Polishing Compound Like wet and dry, there are different products available that are graded by the aggressiveness of the compound. The unit of measurement is G and the number that follows it relates to the coarseness, in the same way it does with production paper – the higher the number, the less aggressive it is. The most commonly used are G3 to G10. A bottle of G3 and G10 should be enough to polish your car.

Machine Polisher There are several different products available – some powered from the mains, some air-fed, and varying in price from £25 to £300.

There are some drawbacks for air-fed units. As the compressed air levels reduce, the speed of the polisher will decrease, which makes it difficult to achieve a consistent finish. They are also less powerful than a mains unit. A good unit from a reputable manufacturer like Rupes will cost around £200, but you can achieve good results from cheaper models. Budget for at least £80. Avoid buying a drill adapter as speed is difficult to regulate and they are hard to balance and control.

DA Sander Foam Heads There are two varieties: compounding foams and polishing foams. Use the compounding foam head after you have applied some compound to your panel to remove any remaining sanding marks. Use the polishing foam head with a finishing product (called machine glaze). Farecla or 3M supply good-quality products.

Air-Fed Dual-Action Palm Sander Instead of moving in a circular motion, DA sanders oscillate, which cuts through the surface more evenly. There is not as much heat transfer when sanding as there is polishing, so there is not as much need for speed regulation and you can take advantage of lighter, cheaper, more compact and manoeuvrable air-fed units. They start at around £50 and go to up to £350 if they are fitted with dust extractors. Cheaper units can bounce when you use them, which means you have less control. But ultimately they are a specialist product and if you only plan on painting one car it may not be worth a large investment.

DA Interface Sponge Pad This is a sponge pad that is attached either by adhesive or Velcro to the DA palm sander, to which you then attach a sanding disc. You should use one each time you use a dual-action sander to prevent panel distortion; it allows enough flex for you to buff in tight nooks and on curved panels without the risk of burning through the paint. You should use Velcro pads where possible, as adhesive interfaces are likely to fail and fly off the polisher.

Sanding Discs For post-paint dry-sanding applications, you should get a box of 1,500-grit discs and 2,000-grit discs. You should ten of each disc.

Water-Misting Bottle This will help lubricate your sandpaper. Buy these new, as used ones may contain products that could react with your paint.

Cleaning Spur These are used to unclog polishing pads when compound builds up.

Razor Blades Use them to remove masking tape and any errant paint. Always use new, sharp blades.

THE FINISHING POLISH

After you have painted your car and made all the necessary corrections to your finished shell, you will need to take a bit more time to give it the final polish it needs to get up to professional standards.

For this reason, investing in a decent dual-action polishing machine is a good idea. Unlike, say, a paint gun, this has a far longer life in your paintwork tool-kit because you can use it to detail your car for years after you have painted it.

Buying your own machine will also give you plenty of time to practise with it. It seems like an easy job – turn on, move over the surface – but you will be using fairly aggressive cutting agents after you have painted, so you should give yourself as much practice as possible on scrap panels before you turn it to your masked, freshly painted car.

And you should leave your masking tape in place, because even at this stage you may have to apply more materials onto the surface. It will rarely be needed after polishing the car, but may be required if you sand your vehicle too aggressively or accidentally burn through a layer of paint, which is an easy mistake to make on tight edges and styling creases in the sheet metal.

It is often staggering how much a machine polish can improve a paint job.

DRY FLATTING

When the car leaves the booth, there will inevitably be a few imperfections in the paint. This is common even for experts. Dry flatting will remove these imperfections and any roughness or orange peel in the texture. Of all the post-paint flatting methods, this is the most aggressive as it is not lubricated and uses a power tool – your DA palm sander – which means there is scope to damage your paint. However, you will use extremely fine sanding discs – between 1,500 and 2,000.

Apply your interface sponge pad onto the DA, then your sanding disc onto that. Start with a coarser 1,500-grit disc, then, one panel at a time, sand from one end and work to the other in methodical lines. Avoid any panel edges or styling creases, as you may burn through to the primer. Stop approximately every 30sec, brush off the sanding dust and check to see if the imperfections have gone.

If you have any concerns about burning through the paint, you can spray a mist of water onto the sanding pad directly, using a water-misting bottle. This is advisable as a precaution if you are sanding curved areas.

WET SANDING

The extent to which you do this is entirely contingent on the paint system you use. Some will only require polishing with heavy cutting compounds, some will have a wet-sanding component and polishing stage in their guidelines – you will need to check to see which is applicable.

As a rule, most enamel paints should not be wet sanded or even polished, because this will damage the outer layer, which acts as a barrier to the layers underneath. It is an extremely antiquated product though, so unless you go out of your way to buy it, you probably will not be using it.

It may sound counter-productive to sand a freshly painted car but – provided your paint system guidelines recommend that you do it – it is a very effective means to achieving a pebble-smooth paint job, and can be used to remedy several imperfections like orange peel, overspray in the top coat and the odd speck of dirt or dust.

Dry flatting should only be undertaken with very fine production paper.

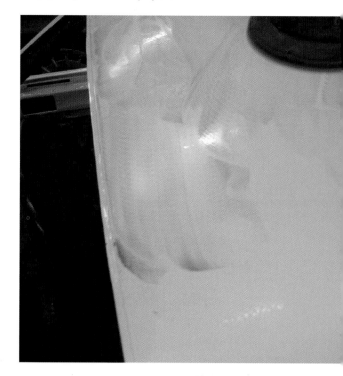

Wet sanding is part of most paint systems.

Chances are, you will not need to wet sand your colour coat, because there are risks that it will damage the tint in the material and leave you with rings and sanding marks that will be visible through the clear coat. Generally, you will only wet sand a clear coat. When the time comes, do not remove your masking tape and paper.

The wet-sanding process does not refer to the use of any old production paper that has been dunked in water. You should only ever use products that clearly state they are suitable for wet and dry applications, else they might be too aggressive or simply fall apart when wet. Specialist products tend to be the very fine paper grades – between 1,500 and 2,500 grit – and are used in a way that differs from the paper you have experienced preparing your body shell.

After wetting the paper for around ten minutes, you will need to apply it to a sanding block. Aim for a maximum width of 5cm (2in) – avoid using anything larger because the imperfections you will deal with tend to be small and localized. When it comes to the sanding itself, be very gentle and avoid using too much pressure – let the paper do the work, and make sure you rinse your paper regularly. This means the panel surface is always wet and ensures that sanding is not too aggressive; it also helps to prevent the paper itself from clogging. You can also add a capful of car wash soap to your bucket to help lubricate the surface, though this is not strictly essential. If you do, check with your paint supplier that it does not contain ingredients that may react with any materials in your paint system.

The reason you should not remove any masked areas is because sometimes, if the imperfection in the clear coat is particularly profound, or you are over-enthusiastic, you may rub through the clear coat completely. This is by no means a cause for concern, but you will need to reapply the lacquer and repeat the process, and if your masking is where you left it, you will not have to do re-do the job.

RIGHT: *Machine polishing skims off the final layer of imperfections.*

POLISHING

Just like wet sanding, machine polishing will not be a suitable for all paints and can even cause damage. You will need to check with the guidelines in your paint to system to see if it is necessary or possible. If you are in any doubt, your paint supplier should be able to clear up any queries.

However, polishing a surface like cured clear coat can add extra depth and shine to your finish, correct paint faults and rub out things like scratches and parking scuffs on your finished car. The task can be undertaken by hand, but more commonly by using a machine polisher. They will spin at fewer revolutions per minute than other DA tools like a sander, cost around £70 and your paint supplier will be able to source one for you.

Providing your paint finish calls for it, you will need to buy some additional supplies to use your machine polisher. You will need a few foam or wool polishing pads – which tend to be attached to the machine with Velcro – some lint-free polishing cloths, as well as the compound itself.

POLISHING COMPOUNDS

Just because it has polish in the name does not mean it works like a wax – waxes are a blend of oils that are absorbed by the paint in the same way your skin would absorb a moisturiser. As well as being completely unsuitable for the job, they can damage fresh paint.

A polish or rubbing compound works very differently. The theory is similar to sandpaper – the liquid has some grit material in it, which flattens the surface smooth. The more coarse the grit, the faster it will flatten the surface, but the more likely it is to leave lesser imperfections on the surface. Because it is available in various grits, you will begin with a coarse compound, then progressively use lighter products until imperfections have completely vanished.

The most likely defect you will encounter is called a swirl mark, which tends to be the result of using a machine polisher, though hand-polishing compounds can also cause the same problems. You should not worry too much about these if you are at the early stages of polishing, because they are usually just the side-effect of dealing with another more serious problem like orange peel or dirt nibs. You will also be able to polish out most of these with either another pass on the area or by using a less coarse compound – it depends on the product you use.

You will find swirl marks are a lot more noticeable on darker colours, but if you are refinishing your car with a lighter colour, it will not be immune to them. Make sure you shine as much light as you can on the area you are polishing, because sometimes these imperfections are only noticeable in bright sunlight.

WHEN TO POLISH

Even if the paint system you use has a hardening agent and looks dry, you will need to be extremely careful to make sure that you have left the correct flash time so all the solvents you applied when painting have evaporated. This information will be supplied with your paint system and varies greatly, so make sure you consult the literature.

At this point, you should keep the car masked just in case you need to reapply paint. It will also protect it from any excess compound, which can stain interior surfaces like vinyl, leather and plastic.

Polishing compounds are not to be confused with car polish.

*Wait until the flash
time has passed
before you polish.*

HOW TO POLISH
WITH A MACHINE

If it is your first time with a power polisher, make sure
you use something that does not spin too quickly,
otherwise you risk burning through the paint. This
can easily happen if you apply too much pressure to
the machine, leave it in the same place for too long or
set it to too high a speed when you polish out edges.

Units are available that spin at a limited 1,450rpm,
which is considerably slower than some heavier duty
machines that spin at up to 3,200rpm. That said, it is
possible for you to make the same mistake using a
low-speed polishing machine.

You should only polish small areas at a time –
around a square meter – and be sure to use any
breaks in the flat surface to define individual sections. Now draw a figure of eight with the compound
onto the middle of a foam or wool-polishing pad,
then evenly dab the pad around the area you wish
to polish.

To avoid your power lead getting in the way of
your polishing job, sling it over your shoulder. And

Polishing machines come in three main sizes.

Polishing a car with a machine.

Avoid power leads getting in the way of your polishing machine.

protect your paint from zips, buttons or loose fibres by wearing an apron. If your polisher has speed adjustment, which most will, use the slowest setting and use the pad to spread the compound around your work area. Once it is on the panel evenly, increase the speed and move the machine either back and forth or up and down the panel in much the same way you did when you were painting, and at much the same speed, overlapping each pass by around 50 per cent. Always keep the machine moving to avoid burning through the paint.

Be particularly careful when you come to a styling crease or edge because this is the area where you will most likely burn through the paint, since the polishing machine will be applying all of its energy and compound onto a very small area. If you are worried about this and there are no major imperfections on the area, you may wish to apply some masking tape and finish by hand.

Remember that some edges, like inner headlight apertures, will be covered in trim, so you should avoid paying too much attention to them with the buffer. Invisible orange peel is infinitely more preferable to bare metal, and the rust problems that could later arise from it.

If you have lots of orange peel in an awkward area that may be susceptible to burning, you can also reduce the speed and attack the imperfection with a slightly reduced risk of burn-through. Be careful, though – if you are in a tight area, be sure there is no single area that is constantly getting polished. If there is no adjustment to the speed of your machine, you can moderate the rpm by switching it on and off in pulses. Generally though, these trickier areas should be finished by hand with a damp cloth and dab of compound.

Never let the pad go dry, and make sure there is always some residual compound on the surface, otherwise you risk deep swirls or burn-through. You will need to clean the pads regularly too. A pad can store a great deal of compound, but there is specialist, inexpensive tool available that will remove any dry material called a pad spur. This clears dry compound from bonnets and foam heads, and fluffs up packed wool. Some cleaning spur tools may also have

Polishing near a styling crease in a panel.

Orange peel paint can be cured with careful polishing.

an abrasive plate, which can restore an even surface to your pad.

Hold the spur up to the pad while it spins, and the old material will fly out. Do not try and do this near the vehicle though, as it will splatter the surface and may damage the paint. If any lands on the surface, remove quickly with a cloth. A spur should level the pad too. You should do this for every four passes, sooner if your pad is visibly clogged. Once you have finished a panel, move on to a new pad. Most are machine washable, but avoid mixing them with ordinary clothes as they can damage them.

Keep polishing and cleaning until the compound has gone and shiny paint remains. You should be able to finish a meter square in around fifteen minutes.

HAND POLISHING

This is a lot simpler than using production paper because it is a lot more difficult to burn through the paint using the strength in your arms alone. But it is a lot more time-consuming and hand polishing should be reserved for small areas that you are unable to reach with a machine polisher, or an area where there is considerable risk of rubbing through.

All you need to do is apply three or four drips to your polishing cloth – never the paint surface – spread it around the panel lightly, then rub it applying a little pressure. Back and forth motions (as opposed to circular) are better by hand as they help you avoid swirl marks.

Hand-polishing a car is safe but time-consuming.

You do not need too much product on your polishing cloth.

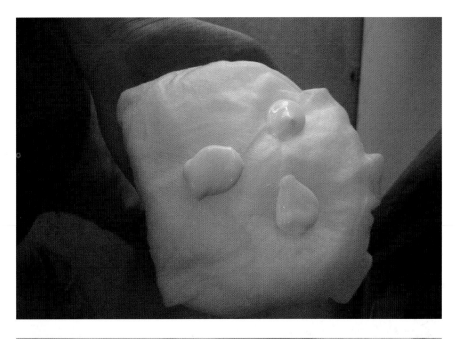

Remove masking tape carefully and have a razor blade available.

REMOVING MASKING TAPE

Once your car is polished to a smooth, shiny surface, you can finally remove your masking tape and reveal your handiwork. Pull tape from the car at an angle away from the painted surface, at as sharp an angle over itself as you can. If you have applied several coats

of coats of paint there is a risk that paint will come off with the tape. This can be a thin and string-like strip, or more serious. By carefully pulling back a little bit of the tape in areas you feel are a risk, you should be able to tell if it is a likelihood. Use a razor blade to cut any errant paint.

Now you can add some additional finishing touches in the next chapter, or move on to reassembly.

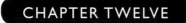

CHAPTER TWELVE

REASSEMBLY

This chapter answers the following questions:

- How should I refit panels (advice regarding rubbers and chrome, mastering panel gaps and how to make adjustments to panel fit)?
- How do I hang on everything else (guidance for windscreen refitting, bumpers, badges and vinyl trim)?

With all of your panels freshly polished, now is the time to start putting your car back together again. This is not a job to be rushed though, especially when it comes to panel gaps. If you do not hang panels onto the shell properly, you risk the panels rubbing together, and with it the paint off your car. Do it right, because this is the last step before the open road.

ASSEMBLY SPECIFICATIONS

You should be able to find a factory manual at either an automotive bookshop, online or through your car club. Inside you will find important techniques, procedures and specifications that will be exclusive to your car. You may find a few useful refitment procedures and shortcuts as well, like where to find hidden alignment holes.

A painted classic car ready for reassembly.

A car being reassembled after paint has been applied.

PANEL GAPS

This phrase relates to the gaps between each panel – this can be between two removable panels, or a panel and the car's monocoque or body. The extent to which these are consistent is based on a great many variables. If you are painting an older car, you will probably need to spend a lot more time making the necessary adjustments, purely because the finish from the factory will have been poor. However, this gives you the opportunity to improve on the original, which will really make your car stand out when you park it next to an unrestored example.

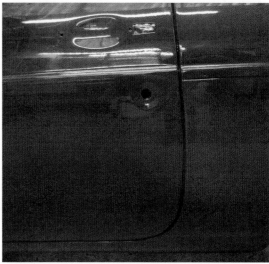

Properly adjusted panel gaps make a huge difference to the appearance of your finished car.

GET THE PERFECT FIT

What you are trying to achieve here is an even and consistent gap between each panel. However, the way this is achieved varies wildly depending on the age of your car and the way it was assembled at the factory. In some cases you need to work from the front backwards, aligning the grille with the radiator, then the shell with the grille and so on. On others, it will be about fitting the doors properly first, then using them as a reference point for the wings, which will then frame the bonnet and grille. But despite the differences, there are some commonalities for proper fitment.

Door Alignment

Always start with a door that is closest to a non-adjustable panel like a rear quarter. For a four-door this will be the rearmost doors. First, you should carefully hang the door on its hinges, and use a door dolly if you can, though a padded scissor jack or similar to support the other end will suffice. Now attach any bolts, but avoid tightening them too much. Everything has to be able to move around until the door is fully aligned.

Carefully line up any styling creases as closely as possible. If you have completely removed everything from the door, like electric window motors and glass, you should refit approximately 1mm above the lines to account for any sag from the additional weight. Tighten the bolts, but not too much as further adjustments will need to be made.

Now everything is in line where the styling creases flow from the rear of the car, you will need to check to see how the door skin fits to the sill. If it is too tight or too far away from the panel, loosen the bolts holding the door onto its lower hinge while either pulling gently with your fingers or pushing with the heel of your hand. Be careful not to bend the metal when you do this.

Closing a gap in one area may open a gap in another, or vice versa. Try and keep the area you have corrected initially as it was, and make your adjustments using the other hinge.

Once everything is where you think it should be, check the door gaps for uniformity. You can afford to be creative here – find something that is not metal and the same size as your desired panel gap and press it in to the gap. You can slide this up and down to check the door fits properly.

Take your time to align doors, as getting the gaps right can help stop water ingress.

Wing Alignment

With your door in place and perfectly aligned to the rear quarter panel of your car, you should either move on to the next door, if it is a saloon, or start attaching a wing. Apply some tape to the door's leading edge to avoid damaging it, and then very loosely bolt it in.

Many front doors will swing open inside the front wing – you should open the door with the wing lightly mounted to check it does not foul the panel. Remember that the door will open wider than it would ordinarily if you have removed the check strap.

If the gap is too wide, you will find the bolts that attach your wing to the bodywork can be tightened to bring the panel in more closely to the car. But you need to be extremely careful not to over-tighten bolts at this stage because it can cause the wings to bow out.

If you are not satisfied with what you are able to do with bolts at this stage, you should use bodywork shims. They fit between the panel and the body so that bolts can be tightened to bring styling lines and gaps together without bowing the metal. Once you have the gaps equal and the lines aligned, use a long, straight edge to check that the wing is not proud of the door.

Bonnet Alignment

This should follow door and wing fitment because each will, in turn, provide a reference point for the next panel. You will have to recruit a helper for this stage, and begin by each taking a side of the bonnet and loosely bolting it to its hinges. This will give you a rough idea of where it sits within the wings.

Make sure the gaps between the bonnet and wings are the same on each side by shimming it, then tighten your bolts. Remember not to worry too much about the height of the bonnet at the front, as this will usually be adjustable with rubber bonnet stoppers. These are threaded into the front slam panel and will allow plenty of adjustment. Just make sure the bonnet still closes in the latch before tightening everything.

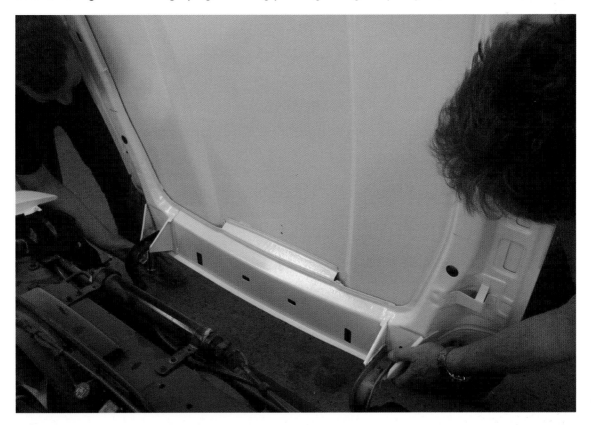

Try and find a helper when you are refitting a bonnet.

Problems with Alignment

This process can take several hours, and you may find that no matter how much you adjust some panels, they simply do not fit together properly. This may be because you used a little too much body filler on your panel. If you are absolutely sure this is the cause, you may need to strip your car back, remove some material and repaint accordingly, for it to fit properly. Remember though, this is an absolute last resort.

GLASS

There are two types of automotive glass – fixed glass and opening glass. Fixed glass is fitted in a way that does not allow it to open, like a windscreen, and opening glass does just that – opens. If you were gunning for the best possible finish, you will have removed both types and the associated rubbers before you embarked on your paint project. But just

as it was with removal, refitting is a tricky job and you will need to be extremely careful, otherwise you risk both shattering the glass and dropping it onto your fresh paint.

If you are concerned about the job, you should leave it to the professionals. Most automotive glass companies are mobile, and will be able to quote you for simple reinstallation jobs, as well as supply new rubbers for your vehicle, regardless of its age. Budget for around £150 for a windscreen, though other panes may vary in price depending on the difficulty of the job and scarcity of the parts.

If you want to have a go at this yourself, it is entirely possible, but if your window rubber shows any sign of deterioration it should be replaced to save yourself a job a few months down the line. Front and rear screen clip and/or rubber replacement is essential, because no matter how new they are, removing the screen may have damaged them, which could cause water ingress and eventually rust.

A classic car windscreen.

GLASS REFITMENT

Just like every other step beyond the paint booth, you should wait for the correct flash time to pass before you start refitting glass. This is because you will need to apply the same masking tape you used when painting your car around the edges of your window frames to avoid any scratches.

At this stage, it is best to consult your owner's manual, because the exact way that your glass fits to your vehicle varies hugely between models. Some may be held in place with a rubber, some may use a rubber and clips, and some may use any combination of these along with a urethane-based adhesive – another reason to ensure you have left the correct flash time.

BUTYL BEAD

You may wish to lay a bead of butyl material between your glass and panel, which will secure the pane in place and could prevent any water leaks. It is an adhesive like some of the urethane materials used at the factory, but is not as strong and should not cause too much of a problem for future removal. If you needed to undertake extensive repairs to any window aperture that could have compromised its shape, you should use this product as a matter of course, as it will fill any gaps that water could reach. If you are using butyl on its own, lay a continuous bead around the window frame.

It can also be used to help along urethane adhesives because it holds the glass in place while the heavier duty material cures. For this application, do not lay down a continuous bead, otherwise the urethane product will not have enough contact to adhere properly. Instead, draw a zig-zag pattern with breaks in, then use urethane to fill the remaining surface.

Remember though, once you have added the urethane, the only way to remove it afterwards is to cut through it with a wire, and if left to an amateur, the job may damage your paint.

GLASS RESTORATION

Companies like Eastwood have started offering kits that use a light polishing compound to get rid of imperfections like hard water spots, mineral deposits, tree sap mist, bugs, paint overspray and oily films.

Eastwood's includes the proper polish and an arbor and buffing wheel for a drill. You may struggle to get rid of scratches deep enough to catch a fingernail on, but it should make a vast improvement on your glass, and the process is very simple.

RUBBER WEATHER STRIPS

If you are refinishing an older car with an unknown history, and providing your budget allows it, you should replace as many rubbers as you can with new items. When you took your car apart you may have noticed some cracking in the seals, but more likely you may have come across some areas where seals had pulled away from their seats, which left a gap. As well as wind noise and drafts, this can lead to water ingress and rust.

While large gaps may look like they have been caused by adhesive failing to do the job – and this may be a contributing factor – it is generally because the seal has shrunk. This tends to happen with age, and regardless of whether or not your rubber is split, it will not seat properly and the problem will persist. Replace any seals showing these signs.

Always buy new window rubbers where possible.

As an absolute minimum, you should replace cracked rubbers.

That said, you should also use some sort of adhesive product to refit rubber. Be careful to choose the right material, though, because anything not entirely right for the job might cause a reaction with your paint, or not work in the tough and varied conditions to which cars can be subjected. If you speak to your paint supplier, they will advise the right tool for the job.

Before you apply any sort of adhesive, make sure you have all the screws or clips ready (though some parts may not require them), and have a good look to see how everything fits together. You may need to use a lever of some sort to properly seat some weatherstrips, but under no circumstances should you use anything metal that may scratch your paint underneath. Plastic tools are available for this purpose, and tend to be very inexpensive.

Once you have fitted the rubbers, lubricate them very lightly with silicon spray. Your original door seals will have been either coated or impregnated

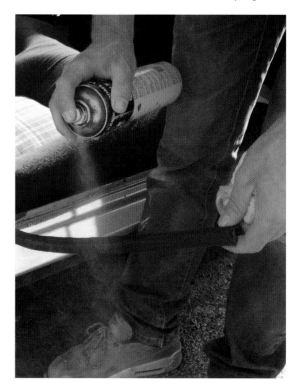

Lubricate door rubbers with silicon spray before you fit them.

Use door rubber adhesive.

with silicone at the factory to stop them binding and squeaking. A lot of replacements parts do not have the coating, which may cause sticking when you open and close the door. Use a light spray of silicone lubricant from an aerosol, but make a quick call to the part and paint supplier to check your paint can stand up to it.

Detailing products for rubber parts are available, but you should wait until you have installed the parts, and for any adhesives to go off before applying them, else the rubber may not adhere to your bodywork properly.

EXTERIOR TRIMS

As you will find when you start hanging trims onto your car, if the parts looked OK when you removed them, they probably look a lot worse against brand new paint. But they can be incredibly expensive to replace, and there are ways to restore their appearance.

PLASTIC TRIMS

First, you should wash them with car shampoo (avoid using washing-up liquid because many varieties contain salt, which could damage your paint) and a soft brush. Once it is dry, you may find that the dirt has gone, but it still looks grey and oxidized. If this is the case try using a machine carpet scrubbing brush on the part. If you speak with your local mobile detailing expert, they may hire you the machine to save you buying one.

Once scrubbed, there are hundreds of different dressing products you can use, which tend to be applied by hand, then buffed off with a clean, soft cloth.

If this still fails to leave a decent finish, you can refinish the parts using special plastic primers and paints. They are available as aerosols, though you can also use them in your spray gun. Your parts will need to be prepared in much the same way your car was

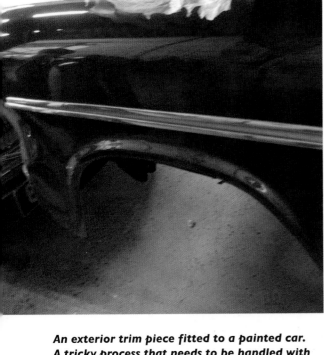

An exterior trim piece fitted to a painted car. A tricky process that needs to be handled with great care.

Use car shampoo to wash your exterior trim.

– clean, degrease, prime, sand, paint, flash time – but because it is far softer, use nothing more coarse than 150-grit production paper to key the primer.

METAL TRIM

Most surfaces can be restored to some extent using a polishing compound, but you will have to determine what type of metal you have before you start polishing. There are several compounds designed to be applied by hand, but they differ depending on the metal itself. All will go some way to restoring the trim, but deep scratches will require either extensive refinishing or replacement. These sorts of metal trims can be expensive to buy new, so consider second-hand items.

You will be surprised how many defects can be removed with a bench-mounted polishing machine and correct use of polishing compounds. The machines themselves cost around £200, though several companies offer a kit that converts a normal 500W bench grinder into a metal polishing machine, which start at a far more reasonable £40. This is a tricky skill to master, though, so it might be worth searching online and finding out where your nearest metal polishing shop is and farming the work out to them.

If you have chrome parts that are dirty or suffering from surface rust, there are several specialist polishing compounds that can restore the finish. Though extremely pitted parts may need to be re-chromed to restore their original shine, or source better second-hand or new parts.

If you have stainless steel parts that are suffering from dents and dings, you would be surprised at how many surface defects, like dents and dings, can be removed with basic metalwork techniques. Unlike chrome, stainless is a very malleable material that does not have a layer you can damage. Lightly reshape these errant parts using the same techniques discussed in Chapter 4, then have them polished, or have a go yourself.

Metal trims may require some special compounds to clean them.

DOOR HANDLES AND LOCKS

On most older cars, your door handles will be made from metal, and some attach directly onto the painted surface. If that is the case, it is worth making a small rubber gasket to sit between the part and paint to avoid chips and scratches. You can buy rubber gasket sheets in various thicknesses, then using chalk, draw an outline around the contact area and cut out neatly with scissors. Make sure the material is oil- and water-resistant to ensure longevity.

Many of these parts will also have factory-supplied gaskets, but you may find that they have become cracked or split with age. Never put these parts back – they tend to be very inexpensive, and if the part is no longer available from your car's dealership, or it isn't remanufactured by an enthusiasts' club, you can make your own with gasket sheet. Without it, you may find that the two metals are incompatible – like aluminium and steel, for example – and may cause a reaction such as galvanic corrosion. This oxidation process occurs from a chemical reaction between two different metals – the weaker of the two will corrode.

FASTENERS

Designers will go to great pains to avoid naked screw heads, nuts and bolts, so many parts like handles will be secured from the inside. Finding them can be difficult – made infinitely less soif you speak to an owners' club – but once you do, make sure that all threads are clean before reinstallation, and avoid over-tightening.

If you are running screws into your paintwork, which may be required to fix several different types of trim, coat heads with some white assembly grease. This puts a layer of protection between the screw and the paint, which prevents the screw blistering or cracking your top coat when it has been full seated. Wipe off any excess grease from around the screw head with a rag.

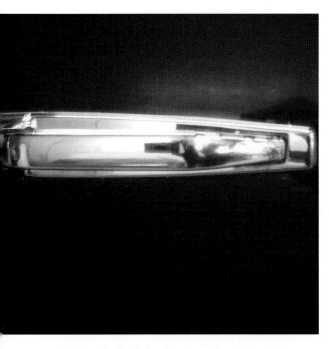

Always replace the gaskets on door handles.

Use assembly grease when applying trim fasteners.

HEADLIGHTS

If you are refitting plastic polycarbonate headlights, you should check to see if the lens shows any signs of oxidization, which gives the lamps a cloudy and yellow appearance and feels slightly rough to the touch. This is caused by a failure of the manufacturer's protective seal, exposing the unit to fine particles hitting it on the road, and UV rays from the sun.

To restore the lenses, find a way to secure them to a bench (do not fit them and expose the car to polishing products if the paint is fresh or you may cause a chemical reaction), and use a light abrasive compound on your polishing machine at slow revs.

If this fails to remove the oxidization, soak a piece of 1,000-grit wet and dry paper in water for ten minutes, then sand in straight strokes following the same direction until all the pits, discolouration and scratches are removed. Now do the same again with 1,500-grit wet and dry in the opposite direction. Then with 2,000-grit wet and dry in the opposite direction, 2,500-grit wet and dry in the other direction and finish with some 3,000 grit in the other direction. Now use your polishing machine and a dab of compound to go over it once more to get rid of all the smaller scratches.

To keep the polycarbonate from re-oxidizing, fit a protective lens film. These can be purchased pre-cut to the shape of your lens. You can also use this process to restore rear plastic light clusters that are damaged from oxidization, but always see if less extreme measures like a simple clean will do the job first – this way you avoid removing any of the manufacturer's protective coatings.

When it comes to refitment, make sure that you have your beam pattern aligned, as you may have disturbed the beam adjusters (two screws next to the headlights that tighten over springs).

Some oxidized headlamp lenses can be fixed.

GRILLES

Generally speaking, most grilles are held in place with screws that tighten into metal clips. You will have to position the clips correctly so that they support the grille, but when they are not tightened with the screws, they can easily slide around and damage your fresh paint. You may wish to use a dab of assembly grease on the inside of the clips – if they do slide around, you will minimize damage this way. Give all the parts you replace a thorough clean before you reinstall before you refit, and if plastic parts have faded, you may wish to respray them with an aerosol.

Plastic and chrome grilles require some refitment.

BUMPERS

On older cars, they can be a cumbersome part to refit, so you may need a helper, or use a support like a padded trolley jack to take the weight of one end. They tend to feature several nuts, bolts and screws as well. Once you are happy with the position of your bumper, pick a side, then go from the outermost fastener and work your way gradually, fastener to fastener, to the other side of the vehicle. Once it is secure, go back the other way and tighten everything fully to the factory specs. Over-tightening at one end can cause it to stick out, so if you have the luxury of a helper, recruit them to push or pull the bumper into position as necessary while you tighten.

Do not over-tighten bumpers.

BADGES AND EMBLEMS

Before you refit any badges and emblems, give them a thorough clean – you will find it a lot easier and will achieve more thorough results with the parts off the car. Using a toothbrush and warm soapy water, scrub the parts to get dirt and polish build-up out of the corners.

If it has a painted section that is chipped or damaged, do not throw it away as you may be able to restore it using touch-up paint and a modeller's brush. Using the tip of a craft knife, see if you can prize up the painted section, though you may need to use paint stripper to fully clean out areas with severely damaged paint. Do not use abrasives though – they will damage the chrome plating beneath the paint. Once removed, clean the emblem thoroughly with paint thinner and wipe them off well with a clean cloth.

With the piece dry, you will notice that the pegs on the back of the badge will make it difficult to lie evenly on a table, so find an old cardboard box, punch holes in where your badge pegs are, then mount the badge to the box so it is level. You may want to use some masking tape to secure it from underneath.

Instead of brushing your paint on, work back and forth transferring small drops of paint to your emblem so that several drops flow together and fill the recessed space – you may need to use thinners to help the material flow properly. By dripping the paint in, you avoid brush strokes appearing in the badge. Let the paint dry overnight and then scrape unwanted material with a small craft knife, then carefully polish the metal with 0000-grade wire wool followed by chrome polish.

REPAIRING SCRIPT BADGES

Chrome-plated metal nameplates that spell out the make or model of your car may have suffered during the paint process. Hasty removal can lead to bent or snapped parts. You should be able to reform it by hand if the part is bent, but snapped badges can cause problems. If it is a clean fracture, use a small grinder or hand tool like a Dremel to run a thin groove in the back of the badge, then use a brass rod of a similar diameter to join the two pieces back together, glued in place with a two-part epoxy adhesive. Once dry, sand the back until it is flat and level, then polish and refit.

With everything refitted and looking factory fresh, you can begin work on the final stage – detailing, then driving.

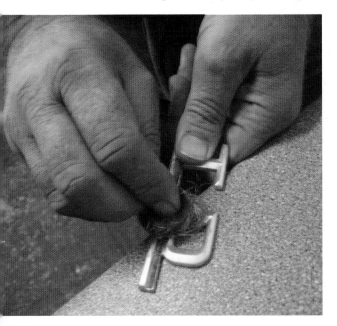

Use 0000-grade wire wool to polish badges.

Bent and snapped badges can be easily repaired.

CHAPTER THIRTEEN

KEEP IT PERFECT

This chapter answers the following questions:

- My new paintwork's been damaged – can I repair it without painting the whole car again (repairing keyed panels, scuffs and minor dents)?
- How can I keep my car looking this good forever (long-term protection, rejuvenate faded paint, what conditions are conducive to keeping paintwork immaculate and how to make the best out of your parking situation)?

You will want your painted car to look as good as it does for as long as possible. Using some clever tips from the detailing world, here are the best ways to keep it looking as good as it did when you first rolled it out of the booth.

MAKE IT PERFECT TO KEEP IT PERFECT

Once you have reassembled your car, hung the chrome and refitted the badges, you need to give your vehicle a proper, deep clean. This is not just a vanity project, though – think of all the sanding you have done to the car, and how much of the dust has gone into the cabin. You can wipe down the surfaces inside, but there is a good chance a lot of it has settled in the car's cabin air system, not to mention the engine bay and harder to reach places.

There is, of course, an element of pride. If you went to all that trouble repairing and repainting your car to such an extensive degree, chances are you will want it to look immaculate, and keep it looking immaculate for as long as possible. Chances are, after all that hard work you will not want to paint your car again any time soon.

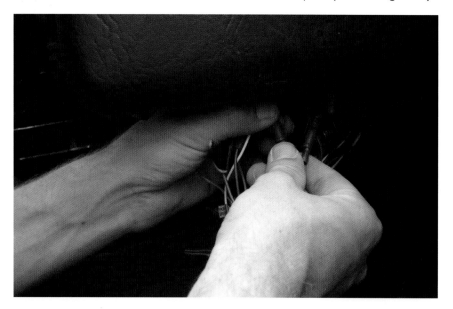

Before you try and fire your car up, check the wiring is re-connected.

PRE-CLEANING

First things first, you need to double-check all of your wiring, making sure that every plug, lead and earth strap you removed has been properly refitted. Now, apply your breathing apparatus and an eye mask, open the windows and, with the engine running, turn your heater blower fan on full, letting it run for about a minute. Because your car has been sitting in a dusty environment, expect a lot of it to shoot out of the vents. Now you can begin cleaning without the risk of blowing filler dust on your freshly prepared interior. Switch off the engine and consider your plan of attack.

NEW PAINT CLEANING CONSIDERATIONS

Detailing and polishing is a science unto itself, with even small car parts' retailers stocking walls of pots, sprays and bottles. And your car probably is not ready for any of them. That is because your paint is not a factory finish.

The differences between DIY and factory finishes are vast, but one of the key considerations is flash time. A new car's paint will be cured in ambient temperatures of up to 140°C (284°F) to speed up the process, and stored for a while prior to delivery, so it can be washed and waxed the day it is delivered. Your paint job relies on a longer curing process, regardless of whether you use heat lamps to speed up the process or not.

You must adhere to all the flash times recommended by your paint manufacturer, otherwise you may inadvertently apply a layer of cleaning product or wax that traps the solvents in the paint.

The paint is also very delicate when it has just come out of the booth, so try and keep it in a cool, dry garage that is as dust-free as possible. Things like dew followed by bright sunshine can leave water spots, dead insects can cause blemishes and bird poo is particularly aggressive. If left for anything more than a few seconds, it can cause major damage while the solvents are gassing out.

Choose your paint cleaning products carefully.

THE SAFE WAY TO CLEAN YOUR FRESHLY PAINTED CAR

There are several cleaning methods that are suitable for fresh paint, but they can only be applied when the bodywork has been thoroughly rinsed, otherwise you risk rubbing gritty dust and grime into the soft, new surface. A thorough hose-down with fresh water should be adequate.

When it comes to cleaning products, a dedicated car shampoo will be suitable, but never use kitchen or laundry products, as they often contain an abrasive that may damage your paint. You should also use a soft cloth or wash mitt, preferably new, to guarantee it does not have any grit trapped in it.

Always work from the top down to stop spreading dirt from the bottom of the car to the top. Also, use a two-bucket system – fill one bucket with water and the appropriate amount of soap, and fill the second with just water. After giving the whole vehicle a thorough rinse with a hose, put your mitt in the soapy water, wash the panel, rinse it in the water-only bucket, then use the soapy bucket again to load up with more cleaning products. That way, any grit gets washed off in the rinse bucket and will not find its way onto your delicate panel. Rinse as frequently as you can, and never let an area go completely dry in direct sunlight, as it may leave water spots. Dry the car with a clean, new microfibre cloth.

Avoid using any dedicated window and glass cleaners at this stage, as they may have chemicals that can react with your new paint.

Use plain water.

POLISHING AFTER
YOU HAVE PAINTED

Once your flash time has passed, now is the time to start applying waxes. As well as giving your car an excellent shine, regular washing and waxing will form a protective barrier between your paint job and everyday contaminants.

Dark colours will need to be waxed more frequently than brighter cars to maintain their gloss because they reflect more light, and you can only wax a washed car. But washing a car removes the wax, so the more you wash, the more you will need to wax. The frequency itself depends on whether or not your car is stored inside or outside, how often it is used and the climate you live in, but there is a simple rule – if you run a clean finger over your paintwork and it squeaks, you should wax it.

BASIC DETAILING SCHEDULE

While there are books dedicated to the subject, following this basic guide will give you an understanding of car care and will help you keep your paintwork in great shape without having to dedicate entire weekends to the endeavour.

Wait until the flash time has passed before applying waxes.

Cleaning your car regularly will increase the longevity of your paint work.

EVALUATE YOUR CAR

Once the car is washed using the two-bucket system and dried using a clean, microfibre cloth, feel the panel with your hand. If it feels in any way rough to the touch, there are contaminants bonded onto the surface that should be removed so your wax works as best it can. This is common even on recently painted cars.

CLAY BAR

Generally speaking, any wax or polishing work will require a fair amount of preparation, and using a clay bar is a great way to do this after your paintwork has been washed. It is best to buy it in a kit, which usually includes a bar of clay, some lubricant and a microfibre cloth. The bar will look and feel like Blu Tak, and just as that picks up dirt when you roll it across a desk, the clay will pick up dirt on your bodywork panels.

To use it, you spray on a mist of lubricant, then wipe the surface with your clay bar – which should be gently warmed and worked in your hands prior to use. Fold it every few passes so you are not rubbing any grit back onto your paintwork. Once you have gone round the entire car, the panels should feel like glass.

WAXING

There are literally thousands of different waxes to choose from, which cost anything from a few pounds to a few thousand, but when it comes to application, it is best done inside a cool, dust-free garage out of direct sunlight, otherwise the product you are using may dry too quickly and may even scratch your paintwork when you try and spread it across the surface of your panels.

What you are trying to achieve – whether you are using a power-polishing mop or a dual-action polishing mop – is a thin, even coating. You have to wait until the wax is dry before you remove it. The easiest way to check this is to run a finger over the surface. If it smears, it is not ready, but if it is clear, you should remove it. Only use a clean, soft, lint-free cloth for this to avoid any scratches, and do not apply too much pressure. You can apply as many as three coats of wax to your car, which should help make your paint as durable as possible. Make sure you do not apply paint waxes to plastic trims, as it can stain them.

Clay bars are an excellent way of removing surface contaminants.

Your choices of wax are vast.

If your wax smears, it is not yet ready for removal.

DEALING WITH IMPERFECTIONS

If you have any swirl marks left on the surface after waxing or washing, chances are some grit or grime has worked its way onto your polishing materials during the washing or waxing process. Provided the scratching has not gone down to the primer of filler, these are removable, or at least easy to disguise.

To understand how this is achieved, it is important to understand the anatomy of a scratch. Imagine a straight line with a V notched underneath it – that is what a fresh scratch looks like at a microscopic level. Light will catch each upper edges of the V and make the scratch obvious. Provided the scratch is not too deep, you should be able to level the paint so it is reaches the lower point of the V using a polishing compound. If the scratch is too deep to completely level, burr the edges of the V to minimize light catching it.

Be wary of some products like T-Cut, as they can be too aggressive for fresh paint; but gentler compounds are fine to use. Also, if you can, use a dual-action polisher like the Meguiar's multi-speed product. At £175 it is an expensive luxury, but does take a great deal of time out of the process.

If the problem is particularly difficult, you can wet sand most scratches out – you will need a power polisher. You should be extremely careful at this stage, because it easy to damage the paintwork more if you use the wrong materials. Begin with a 3,000-grit wet and dry paper that has been soaked in water for at least 15min. You can also add a dash of car shampoo in the bucket to help lubricate it. After you have wet the panel, use a plastic or rubber sanding block to avoid damaging the paint further, then gently apply straight line motions to the panel. Straight sanding marks are a lot easier to buff out, so avoid any circular motions. Sand for 8–10min until the defect is gone, constantly lubricating the surface with a misting bottle full of clean water. Now use a power polisher to get rid of the sanding marks. Make sure your polishing pad is applied evenly onto the polisher's backing pad so no part of it comes into contact with your panel.

Avoid T-Cut as it is too aggressive for fresh paint.

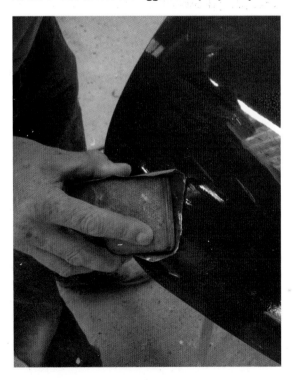

You can sometimes wet sand a scratch out of fresh paint.

POLISHING PADS

There are, in effect, two different types of pads to choose from for power polishing, regardless of whether it is after wet sanding or as a first solution: wool and foam. Wool acts as an additional abrasive, which is good for removing deeper imperfections, and will remove sanding marks if you use a more aggressive wet and dry paper, like 1,500 grit. Foam pads should be used to get rid of 2,000-grit scratches. Be careful not to run a powerful polisher too fast – between 1,500 and 2,000rpm should do it – as it may burn the paint. Also, make sure each pad is flat onto the surface to ensure the heat is spread over the pad's intended surface area. Use a clean foam pad by removing from the panel, running the buffer and holding a nylon brush onto it. Use a spur to clean wool pads.

There are two major polishing pads to choose from: wool and foam.

Using a hole punch allows you to quickly remove a small disc.

REPAIRING STONE CHIPS

It is an inevitability that you will pick up a few stone-chips, if you use your freshly painted car regularly. However, if they are not down to the bare metal, you should try repairing them by wet sanding the area and polishing as above, as it is a difficult problem to disguise.

That said, if it is down to bare metal, it should be repaired immediately to avoid corrosion forming. You will need to check with your paint supplier to see which products will be compatible with your system, and you will also need the colour code from the paint you used (though ideally you will have some of the paint you used to finish the car originally left over).

Use a hole punch on some 2,000-grit production paper and then remove the circular piece from the punch's waste tray. Superglue it on to the rubber end of a pencil and, using your forefinger and thumb, dry sand the area where your chip has formed, scuffing as little of the surrounding paint as possible. You do not

need to take the area down to bare metal, but flatten bumpy paint and give the paint something to bite to.

Now apply a light layer of car wax onto the surrounding area and, using a cotton bud, remove the wax from the bare metal chip itself with some thinners. This avoids you getting touch-up paint on areas of the car that do not need it, which helps make the repair as invisible as possible. It also means that any accidental drips can be cleaned away easily.

Depending on the system you are using, you should now mix your paint. Because it is a small repair and you need the product to be as workable as possible, go for a half-and-half ratio of paint and clear coat.

Take another cotton bud, remove the end and sharpen the plastic to a point. Dip it into the paint, then carefully dab it onto the bare metal. You can speed up the drying process by using a heat gun for about five minutes (but do not let the surrounding panel get too hot). Remember that the paint will contract, so you will probably need to add additional layers of touch-up.

Thinner and paint ready to stir.

Between each application, wet sand the area with 2,000-grit wet and dry until there is no trace of bare metal and the paint is level with the rest of the surface. Be careful that the paint you are using to apply to the chip does dry while you are making these repairs, and always mix up a new batch if you are not sure. Paint should survive for around 15min in the open air before it needs to be replaced.

Once you are happy that the bare metal has been completely coated, remove the sanding marks and level the paint using the techniques and products detailed above. You may have to repeat this process several times before it looks as good as new. Once you have finished, you should wax your car for protection.

COLOUR MATCHING AND BLENDING

If you have had a small accident that has significantly damaged the paintwork, you may be able to repair the panel, repaint it and blend it into the rest of the car. But not only will you have to find a close match for the paint itself, you will also have to blend in the old with the new, which requires a degree of refinishing to both damaged and undamaged panels.

The rules and principles outlined earlier in the book that relate to masking, paint compatibility, appropriate working areas, necessary safety equipment and flash times, remain the same. However, after you have made all the necessary repairs and are happy with what has been carried out, you will have to prepare your panel slightly differently.

DEFINE YOUR AREA

First you need to choose an area that will help you to best disguise the fact that you have made a repair. You have two options in this instance: mask up to a panel line or other definite edge, or things like a pronounced styling crease, pinstripe or graphic. In theory, providing your paint supplier has given you an accurate colour match, the repair should meld neatly with your original respray. Using the practices defined in earlier chapters, prepare the affected panel and repaint it.

PAINT AN ENTIRE SIDE

Single-panel painting comes unstuck if there is the tiniest difference in the colour provided and the colour on your car. This could be a very small change in the paint mixing process or it could be your car's exposure to sunshine, which – even within a few

Be careful when painting a single side of your car.

months in some climates – can cause the colour itself to fade. If this is the case, and your vehicle is a lighter shade like silver (one of the hardest colours to match), painting up to a panel line will exacerbate the contrast, and make the repair painfully obvious.

If you have concerns that your paint has faded in any way, or you would rather write yourself an insurance policy that reduces the effect of a colour change, it is recommended that you paint the whole side of the car that is affected. It may seem like over-kill, but this procedure is recommended by paint manufacturers, especially if you have painted the car using a custom, candy or pearl paint job, because they are so hard to match.

There is also the matter of matching up the paint itself. Not only could the rest of the car be faded, it may also have suffered from oxidation – this ensures that there will be continuity between an entire side of the car, from front to back. Once you have finished painting and allowed it to dry thoroughly, you should machine polish the whole car to restore the original paint as best you can.

Just repairing a single door can lead to colour match issues.

MELT IN THE NEW FINISH

There is an alternative solution to painting the entire vehicle. It seems counter-intuitive, but if you are repainting, say, a front door on a saloon car, you can repaint an area up to the middle of the adjacent rear door, and 'melt' in the new finish with the old. This technique is a little more advanced, but can be mastered with some practice and will hide your repair far more successfully.

You will need a special product called paint blender. It works on single-stage paints, which do not require a clear coat. That means it is compatible with several original paint finishes on older vehicles (but always check that it is compatible with your system – your paint supplier will be able to give you this information). Basically, the product prevents the halo effect you are likely to see surrounding the outside edges of a local repair once the clear coat has dried, which clearly shows a dividing line between old and new paint. The blender literally blends in old and new paint together with solvents.

Simply apply your clear coat in the normal fashion and while the final coat is still wet, mist the blender around the outside edges of the repair. As it dries, the blender will begin to 'melt' the repaired edges into your car's existing paint, leaving you with a spotless finish that looks like new. It is available as a stand-alone aerosol product or as a mixer for your paint. The latter is preferable, as you will have far more control using a dedicated, well set-up paint gun, but always check its compatibility with your paint supplier. If it is not suitable, you will cause further damage to your paint.

This method requires less surface area of your vehicle to be prepared – it can be as little as 12cm (5in) around the affected area – because you are blending in, as opposed to completely repainting. Once the damaged areas have been repaired, primed, block-sanded with 320-grit production paper, given a guide coat to check for 320-grit scratches, rubbed down with 600-grit production paper, scuffed the entire blend area and degreased, you can begin masking the panel. You may also wish to wet-sand the area where you intend to make your blend, to soften the plaint slightly and further reduce the halo effect.

You should cover all the bodywork that does not require a repair that is 25cm (10in) away from the affected area – you will still be creating overspray, so thorough masking is required to avoid making extra work for yourself in the buffing stage, or even damaging the original paint.

For blending work, you can also use masking tape to help you along. Instead of applying it as you would do to protect something from paint, you should use some 2in tape, only using half of the long edge's adhesive. Roll the tape back on itself until the edge of your work area is exposed, then pin it back with small tabs of tape. This gives you a soft paint edge, instead a firm line paint that would be achieved by using the material normally.

Products do vary in terms of application, but something from a quality brand like DuPont will initially require you to paint the areas as you would normally. Once the colour has been applied, roll the reverse tape edge back slightly further so that the soft edge of paint is melted down at the same time as the paint in the main area you are repairing. Once you have done this, mix the blender 1 to 1 with the mixed paint for the last coat of urethane colour or clear coat.

You will need to step the paint/blender mix beyond the last layer of colour or clear coat you have sprayed on. Now, after either thoroughly cleaning your gun or using a pre-cleaned unit, spray the neat blending product on just the outer edges to melt them in. Be careful at this stage, because blending agents run extremely easily, so make sure your air pressure is as low as possible.

Once dry, and with all of your masking tape and paper removed, buff the blended area first to remove the shop-fresh shine, then buff the entire area.

As with all localized repairs, this method is not as hardwearing as a full panel spray job, but if enough care is taken of the vehicle and the affected area, it can last well.

Paint blender can help match colours.

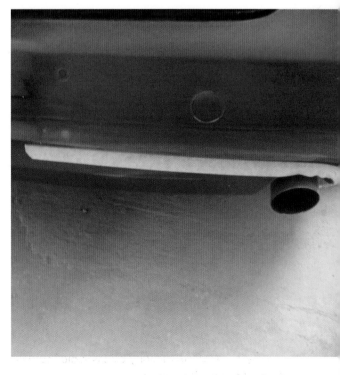

Preparing a small area for blending.

You should still mask the rest of the car.

Turning down the air pressure on your gun to get the best blend.

CONCLUSION

Now you have the skills to strip, repair and paint your car – and keep it looking perfect forever. Go for a drive and enjoy the fruits of your labour. There is, however, great scope to expand your restoration skills beyond just painting. Additional titles from Crowood, include *Welding – A Practical Guide to Joining Metals*, as well as the more spe-

cific, specialist title *Wooden-Bodied Vehicles – Buying, Building, Restoring and Maintaining*.

That said, if you have at this point painted your vehicle, you should enjoy driving your car and feel great pride in having done the job yourself. It involves skills that require great patience and, more often than not, a fair bit of trial and error due to the vast difference not just between marques, makes and models, but from one car to the next.

INDEX